HOW TO THINK LIKE A WRITER

For Creative Writing Students and Their Tutors

LOUISE TONDEUR

Copyright © by Louise Tondeur

First published 2017

Revised edition 2022

All rights reserved.

No part of this book may be reproduced in any form or by any electronic or mechanical means, including information storage and retrieval systems, without written permission from the author.

Greetings from the (sometimes) sunny south coast

Why you should read this book

Hi. I'm Lou. I'm a writer and a writing tutor. I live on the sometimes sunny south coast of England. A few years back I wrote the first 'small steps guide' and in *How to Think Like a Writer* I apply exactly the same ideas to learning and teaching Creative Writing, resulting in a set of accessible, tried-and-tested techniques that you can learn (and teach) easily – simply by taking small steps.

All of the Small Steps Writing Guides are based on two principles. One, you can take any big project, goal or task, like learning more about the 'creative' part of Creative Writing, and break it down into smaller and smaller steps until it becomes doable. Two, if you take small but *specific* actions towards your goals regularly enough, they'll have a snowball effect. That means that with help from *How to Think Like a Writer* you and your students can start taking small steps towards developing your writing practice.

Greetings from the (sometimes) sunny south coast

A free course and practical advice

Sign up to my mailing list over on my website here https://www.louisetondeur.co.uk to get a free video course on Writing and Mindset. You can find out more about my other books and courses by following the links from here: https://www.louisetondeur.co.uk/work-with-me/ And get advice and guidance on the writing life from my blog, including resources for teachers and lecturers.

Contents

Introduction	vii

Part I
Your Writing Toolkit

Week One: Get Writing	3
Week Two: Keep Writing	6
Week Three: Freewriting	10
Weeks Four: Close Observation	17
Week Five: Creative Visualisation	30
Week Six: Writing Props	43
Week Seven: Live Writing	52
Week Eight: Wordplay	58
Week Nine: Mindfulness	63
Week Ten: Can Creative Writing Be Taught?	72

Part II
Developing your practice

Week One - Three: Creative Journeys	85
Week Four: Processes	92
Week Five: Storyboarding	97
Week Six: Rewriting the Myths of Success and Failure	102
Week Seven to Ten: The Journey from Idea to Bookshelf	107
How to Organise a Literary Event	113

Part III
Living as a Writer

A Creative Careers Workshop	129
How to Find a Writing Job	138

Acknowledgments	147
About the Author	149
Also by Louise Tondeur	151

Introduction

Who is this book for?

This book is aimed at Creative Writing undergraduate and postgraduate students and their tutors. If you're a student you can work through the prompts on your own alongside your course, or your tutor may incorporate them into seminars and workshops. It also works as a course of two x ten weeks.

If you are a writer who is not on a course, the tools in this book will help you develop your writing practice, and will act as a DIY writing course if you like.

What is this book about?

This centres on the relationship between mindfulness and mindset and practical writing advice. A lot of books claim to teach your how to write, that is, they teach you about the nuts and bolts of a good sentence, or a good story, or they give you a set of writing prompts to try. I've written a couple of these myself. This book is different because it's about *thinking* like a writer. Am I really going to tell you how to think? No – definitely not – read on and you'll find out why.

This book is also about being a writer in the world, and what it means to follow a creative career path in a sociocultural environment that's often trying to stop us. More on that in part three.

What do you mean by 'how to think like a writer'?

You are a writer if you have made a habit out of writing. Full stop. You're in the right place if you want to learn more about that habit. A more correct title for this book (though a bit of a mouthful) would be *how to think like the writer you already are*. This book isn't going to tell you how to think, instead it's going to ask you to think about how you write, how you create, and how you think creatively, and you'll get lots of practical activities to try out along the way.

Here's one now: if time and money were no object, what would you write? How often? Where would you write? Make a note. No-one else has to see. Now try this. Wherever you are right now, really notice what's in front of you, where you are sitting, and what you can hear. Write it down.

Often the world around us doesn't encourage us to be creative, so we can end up confused about how to carry out our writing practice. Owning a creator mindset – in a nutshell we're observers of the details that other people miss – can feel overwhelming. How do we think creatively without the overwhelm? By reading this book and acting on the advice, you (or your students) will discover a portable writers' toolkit that you can adapt for your own devices, that will make the process a whole lot easier to manage.

In other words: both making a habit out of writing and owning the creator – or specifically the writer's – mindset can be hard, given the world we live in, so here's some help.

Important themes in this book

1. *Connecting with your own creativity.* This sounds quite jargonistic, and I suppose it is until you actually do it, for real. The most important words in the phrase 'connecting with your own creativity' are 'your own'. It helps to know about how other people get creative, but ultimately you're on your own journey of discovery here. You'll discover what you do when you're 'being creative' by experimenting and breaking down the process.
2. *Creative tools.* You'll get a set of tools to use called a 'writer's toolkit'. Try them out. Adapt them. Continue to use them if they work for you, and make them part of your practice; rework them or abandon them if they don't.
3. *Practice.* Creative practice is a habit – so it's important to get into the *habit* of using the tools in this book. Take practice more literally too: practise these tools, with a spirit of curiosity, experimentation and trial and error, as an antidote to self-blame, perfectionism and impatience.
4. *The internal censor or 'the judge'.* The concept comes from Dorothea Brande's *Becoming a Writer*

(Brande, 1981: 56). You'll come across the idea of 'avoiding your internal censor or judge' a few times in this book. This is the voice that tells you to give up, that you're not a writer, that your writing is rubbish. We start to get in touch with our writing voice when we accept (and then ignore) this internal censor.

5. *Being deliberate.* This means deliberately trying out creative strategies as a way of pushing against the internal censor and society's pressure to 'fit in' and find a 'proper job'. (Actually, even this is a truism, because there are plenty of so-called 'proper' jobs that use a whole heap of creative thinking, writing and communication skills.) More on this kind of pressure in a moment.

6. *Encountering the world.* Going for walks, getting out and about or engaging with the world around you somehow is important for connecting with your creativity. This book is definitely not simply about sitting writing at a computer. If you can't get outside, go to interesting places in your imagination or use portals like doors and windows or snatches of overheard conversation.

7. *The Journey.* We could describe the writing life, the process of writing and the shape of a book using a journey metaphor. How helpful is this metaphor and how do we use it to our best advantage?

8. *Reflecting on the process.* Creative Writing students are often asked to write reflectively about their work. What should you write? What does reflection mean anyway?

Introduction

9. *Teaching Creative Writing.* Is it possible to teach someone else to be creative or to write creatively? As we're tutors or students involved in the Creative Writing game, it is helpful to understand the interactions and transactions involved in teaching and learning creativity. You'll get several opportunities to try teaching others to be creative if you're working in a group.
10. *Creative Careers.* How is a freelance writing career different from other life paths? What preparations can you make now? What small steps can you take today? In part three, you'll get some practical suggestions.

These themes are repeated and embellished throughout, to invite you to go deeper, but you might have already noticed that the overriding theme in this book, one that underpins all of the others, is YOU.

What is a writer's toolkit?

A writer's toolkit is a set of tools that you can use in your writing practice to help you to generate words, and connect with your creative side. These are creative tools that you practise over and over, deliberately, which help you to both accept and confront your internal censor / judge.

The other reason to develop a writer's toolkit is because it's portable. You can carry it with you to each creative project you embark on. You can adapt and use the toolkit for *any* creative work. Idea generation is an extremely useful side effect, but it isn't the toolkit's main purpose.

It's worth emphasising that there's something about

Introduction

contemporary culture that tries to stop us from living a creative life. Almost all creative people will have come up against this – from inside themselves, from those close to them, from the attitudes of others. We seem to get the message that we should stay safe, and that being creative is too risky, and not a 'proper' way to live. Therefore it can feel like we're pushing against the tide.

The toolkit is a deliberate answer back to these implicit or overt pressures. They are often undefined but are leveraged as a way to try to stop us practising, to stop us being creative, or to stop us observing the world through a writer's eyes.

Your toolkit will almost certainly be different from mine, and I'd love to hear more about the tools you use. For now, I'm going to tell you about the tools I've found the most useful. They are freewriting, close observation, creative visualisation, live writing, writing props, wordplay, and mindfulness for writers. You'll spend a week or more on each one as you work through the book. I've explained them briefly below.

- Freewriting: writing without stopping, without editing, without necessarily making sense.
- Creative Visualisation: holding a picture in your head, then describing it. Or: using the senses to describe a person, place or thing.
- Close Observation: watching something very closely for a period of time OR noticing the detail in your everyday life.
- Writing Props: Writing *prompts* are starting points or stimuli for your writing. They refer to any image, line of text, place, or game (etc.) that gets you started. However, coming from a Drama teaching background, I tend to

emphasise the use of objects or 'props' as prompts in my workshops.
- Live Writing: writing while in an interesting or unusual place, improvising on the spot. This tool also gets called 'Writing in Situ' or 'immersive writing.' The objective correlative is important; in particular, we associate an emotion with the place that we're in.
- Wordplay: returning to (seemingly) childlike playing, to generate ideas. Messing around with words using games.
- Mindfulness: being aware of the moment, the opposite of striving towards the future. Pausing to look. Noticing the world around us.

And finally, there's an extra tool: Exploring Writers' Venues. That is, being a 'literary citizen' (Friedman 2018), hanging out in particular places that are dedicated to writing or one aspect of it, on or offline. Try to find out about writing organisations, events, festivals, and online spaces as you work through this book. Those might be cafés, libraries, community centres, bookshops, writing organisations, retreats, performance venues, or any places / online spaces where writers come together.

Start with a notebook

Get hold of a notebook that you can love; not too precious you're afraid to write in it, not too fly away, and in a layout you prefer, but not just an A4 pad. For instance, I like A5, side-opening notebooks. Carry your notebook with you and use it for the activities in this book. You could create a digital notebook on a computer, or record your thoughts on a Dictaphone, or the digital equivalent, although there is something special about a notebook that is physical and handwritten.

If you can't imagine using a handwritten notebook, then create a digital one and keep a physical scrapbook or box file instead, placing ephemera or found text and images inside it. Alternatively, challenge yourself to treat a physical notebook as something completely different – a thing to write for its own sake.

How to use your notebook

However you do it, keep a notebook near you. In it, write down any thoughts, ideas, dreams, lines of dialogue, recipes, proverbs, bits of plot, lists of words, poems, definitions, descriptions, postcards, 'live writing' exercises, flights of fantasy, characters, observations and word pictures that you would like to save. Experiment with new writing exercises in it. You can do this using an 'objet trouvé approach'; it doesn't have to be neat. In fact it's better if it isn't, unless neat is important to you. It can also contain images – your own or those you've found – if you would like.

It can be a record of particular walks around your local area or further afield or destination-less wanderings, like a flâneur's journal. Your notebook is useful for collecting dialogue and discovering how people really speak (we almost never speak in full sentences or say what we mean).

Some writers distinguish between a journal in which they record dreams, thoughts, and memories, and a notebook that they carry around with them or use at their desk. Some combine the two. Some (like me) fill up lots and lots of the latter everything-type notebooks. The main thing is: keep it to yourself so that you feel it is yours.

Introduction

The notebook as a sanctuary

Return to your notebook in hectic moments, when you need some calm. Take it with you to quiet places – even if it's only for a few moments – so you can get away from it all and write in peace. I take mine on train journeys. If possible take this notebook into contrasting environments at least once a month – particularly those that change over time. Take your notebook to a café or a beach at different times of day, for instance, as this will really help with the writing process. Go in your imagination if you can't get out and about.

Use your notebook to think about how your writing is going, and to reflect on how you are using it, and what has come out of it. Are there any sections which you could turn into something else or use in a story or poem you are writing, for example?

A note about weeks

Please go at your own pace – this is about your creative process. However, I've divided this book into weeks rather than chapters, to give you a sense of what to do when, and so that the Creative Writing tutors amongst you can turn this book into two ten week courses. I have also added a summary of what goes on in a chapter at the end of each to help tutors with planning. Here are your two ten week courses:

Your Writing Toolkit

- Week One: Get Writing
- Week Two: Keep Writing

- Week Three: Freewriting
- Week Four: Close Observation
- Week Five: Creative Visualisation
- Week Six: Writing Props
- Week Seven: Live Writing
- Week Eight: Wordplay
- Week Nine: Mindfulness
- Week Ten: Can Creative Writing Be Taught?

Developing Your Practice

- Week One: Prepare for your Creative Journey
- Week Two: Go on your Creative Journey
- Week Three: Reflect on your Creative Journey
- Week Four: Processes
- Week Five: Storyboarding
- Week Six: Rewriting the Myths of Success and Failure
- Week Seven: Publishing an anthology of student work (1)
- Week Eight: Publishing an anthology of student work (2)
- Week Nine: Publishing an anthology of student work (3)
- Week Ten: Publishing an anthology of student work (4)
- Extra workshop: Creative Careers

Download the course plan from here: www.louisetondeur.co.uk/how-to-think-like-a-writer-for-creative-writing-students-and-tutors/download-your-course-plan-here

Introduction

Discussion

Because Creative Writing students will be using this book in class, I've included questions for group discussion at the end of each chapter. If you are working through this book with a group, this is your chance to go in depth about some of the themes and ideas, and to hear what people around you think.

Want more?

Throughout this book I will recommend other resources you can access to find out more about a particular topic. For example, if you want to follow up on the ideas in this chapter, you could take a look at Ralph Fletcher's *Breathing in, Breathing out*, Julia Cameron's *The Artist's Way* or *The Sound of Paper* or Dorothea Brande's *Becoming a Writer*.

Summary of the introduction

This book is about being a writer in the world or *how to think like the writer you already are*. It's a practical guide to *making a habit out of writing and owning the creator mindset*. This book is aimed at Creative Writing students and Creative Writing tutors, but individual writers will find it useful too. The ten main themes – ideas repeated throughout for emphasis – are connecting with your own creativity, creative tools, practice, the internal censor or judge, being deliberate, encountering the world, the journey, reflecting on the process, teaching Creative Writing, and Creative Careers.

The writer's toolkit is a set of tools that you can use in your writing practice. It's called a toolkit because it's portable. Your toolkit will most likely be different from mine. Here are the seven tools included in this book: Freewriting, Creative Visualisation, Close Observation, Writing Props, Live Writing, Wordplay and Mindfulness, plus an extra one: Exploring Writers' Venues. Your über tool is your notebook: get hold of a notebook that you can love and use it for the activities in this book. Carry it with you. This book translates into a two x ten week course. Please adapt the advice and activities for your own purposes.

Works Cited

Brande, Dorothea. *Becoming a Writer*. Tarcher, 1981.

Cameron, Julia. *The Sound of Paper: Inspiration and Practical Guidance for Starting the Creative Process*. Penguin, 2006.

Cameron, Julia. *The Artist's Way: The Spiritual Path to Higher Creativity*. Pan, 1995.

Fletcher, Ralph. *Breathing in, Breathing out: Keeping a Writer's Notebook*. Heinemann, 1996.

Friedman, Jane. *The Business of Being a Writer*. University of Chicago Press, 2018.

PART I

Your Writing Toolkit

Week One: Get Writing

Dive straight in with some practical activities

The first couple of weeks are practical and experimental. You're going to have a go at some writing activities. Make a habit out of them just for a couple of weeks, in a spirit of openness and curiosity. If something doesn't work first time, try it again, and be prepared to report back if you're in a group.

The reason you're doing this at the get go, rather than reading an explanation, is that it is easier to understand this set of creative tools by doing them. Try them out, adapting if necessary, to see if they work for you. Be especially open and curious to activities that you feel resistance to, just for the time being. You don't have to continue with them. Over the next week, try any or all of these exercises:

Freewriting:

- Write for one minute without stopping.

- Try again, this time for five minutes.
- Try again, this time for ten minutes.

Creative Visualisation

- Close your eyes.
- Hold the image of an apple in your head.
- Use all of the senses available to you. Fill in the detail.
- Imagine taking a bite.

Repeat this exercise until you can see and taste the apple clearly, feel it in your hand, smell it and hear the crunch when you bite it. If you find visualisation doesn't work for you, concentrate on writing through the senses instead. Describe an apple as accurately as possible using all of your senses.

Close Observation

- Listen to a piece of music. After the music has finished, write about it.
- Find objects of different textures. Everyday objects are best. Write about the textures of the objects.
- Observe an object for fifteen (or 5 or 30 or 45) minutes. After the observation, write down what you experienced.
- Look back over what you've done. Underline any phrases or images which you particularly like.

Discussion

- What do we mean when we talk about 'thinking like a writer' or 'thinking as a writer'?
- Do writers think differently from other people?
- Do you have your notebook yet?
- How did you choose it and why?

Want more?

Read the short section on freewriting at the beginning of Peter Elbow's book *Writing with Power*.

Summary of week one

You've had a go at some gentle 'starting off' exercises, because it's easier to learn them by doing than by reading about them first. For example, try writing for one minute without stopping, or observing an object for a set amount of time before writing down what you experienced.

Works Cited

Elbow, Peter. *Writing with Power: Techniques for Mastering the Writing Process*. Oxford University Press, 1998.

Week Two: Keep Writing

How Week Two Works

As you did in Week One, you're going to spend some time doing a range of practical activities this week, so you've had a taster of each of the techniques we're going to use across this book before we get into the details.

Writing Props

- Make a list of objects or gather some objects together.
- If you're doing this exercise with other people, swap lists or objects with someone else.
- Take one of the objects and ask 'what if?' What if someone found the object lying in the road? Write about it.

Live Writing

1. Think about the place you are in right now. Your seat, your clothes, whether you're warm or cold, the taste in your mouth, what you can smell, see and hear. Experience the place you are in as fully as possible using as many senses as you can. Focus on the details. If you were going to write about the place you are in right now, what words would you use? Write for five minutes. If you're without one or more of your senses adapt the activity to suit.
2. Repeat this exercise but this time go somewhere outside to do it, or go there in your imagination. Walk around the block or go to a café.
3. Go to a particular place. Imagine a (made up) character in the place. Give them a reason for being there. Describe something you can see for five minutes without stopping, *as if you were that person.* As before, visit in your imagination if you can't go in person.

Word play

Play word association with a friend or trying playing it with yourself. Make lists of random nouns, verbs and adjectives and put them together in interesting ways. Make a list of types of food. (Swap lists with someone if you can.) Describe the food using lots of specific detail, making it as colourful, strange and wonderful as possible.

Writers' Venues

Research and visit a writers' venue near you or find a virtual writing community online to visit.

Discussion

- What do you think is meant by the term 'literary citizen'?
- Why is 'playing' important as a writer?
- What's the point of writing prompts? Why use *props* as prompts?
- Discuss the provenance of a particular object.
- Did you visit any writers' venues in person or online? Swap your findings.

'Literary citizen' is a term coined by Rob Spillman, former editor of Tin House, and referenced by Jane Friedman in *The Business of Being a Writer*, p. 19.

Want more?

Find several books of writing prompts to review and recommend to others. Have a look at the section on 'play' in Rob Pope's book *Creativity*, or at the beginning of Jane Friedman's *The Business of Being a Writer*.

Summary of week two

You've had a go at a series of writing activities, getting a taster of 'writing props,' 'live writing,' 'word play' before we get into the details. You've also had the opportunity to explore writers' venues on and offline, and to discuss literary citizenship.

Works Cited

Friedman, Jane. *The Business of Being a Writer*. University of Chicago Press, 2018.

Pope, Rob. *Creativity: Theory, History, Practice*. Routledge, 2005.

Week Three: Freewriting

What is Freewriting?

Many practitioners, such as Julia Cameron and Natalie Goldberg, advise us to use this tool; it gets called different things like 'jumbled writing' or 'writing without stopping' or 'improvisation' or 'stream of consciousness'. Peter Elbow calls it 'freewriting' (Elbow 1998: 13). Essentially it involves writing down what is in your head without thinking too much about it first.

Freewriting brings out interesting ideas, phrases, characters, and situations that you can develop in a more substantial (and later, edited) piece of writing. Sometimes freewriting is like method acting – we write in role as a fictional character. There are various versions of freewriting: some where you get a prompt to start you off, others where you simply write for a set amount of time.

A note about stream of consciousness

When we talk about 'stream of consciousness' as a literary technique we mean writing that has been edited to read as though we are hearing the inner thoughts of a character.

Famous examples are *Mrs Dalloway* by Virginia Woolf and *Ulysses* by James Joyce. This is very different to the writing technique we're using here because when we use freewriting we deliberately do not edit as we go. One is highly stylised, the other is not.

How do you do it?

When freewriting, the only real rules are 'don't think first' and 'keep going'. Move your pen or keep typing. Even if you write the same word over and over, keep writing. Don't evaluate, don't cross anything out. You don't have to spell correctly or punctuate. Save that for the redrafting. If you're writing by hand, you don't have to be neat, or even write on the lines or make sense.

Write the first thing that comes into your head. Be brave. Often freewriting is the first time we've been 'allowed' to write like this without worrying about neatness – it can feel liberating but also hard to let go at first. Keep practising.

Freewriting is a way of getting past the inner censor / judge, a way of starting, a warm up, a form of self-expression, a space to play. and a source of ideas, inspiration, characters and stories. Some writers use it as a kind of meditation, or a ritual to launch them into their work.

I've taught students for whom freewriting has been epiphanic and others who hate it! Try it and see.

The Internal Censor or Judge

All of the writing tools in this book are designed to help us overcome our internal censor or judge in some way. As I mentioned in the introduction, this is the critical voice inside us that tells us we're not 'real' writers, we should give up or that our writing is terrible.

Every creative person has a critical voice like this. Dorothea Brande calls it 'the judge in oneself' (Brande, 1981: 56). Natalie Goldberg describes it as 'the editor' and 'an old drunk fool' (Goldberg, 2005: 28). Ted Hughes called it our 'inner police system' (Cope 1986: 5). We can't escape this judge or push it away, but we can examine it, accept it, confront it, laugh at it, and keep writing anyway.

There are a couple of reasons why we need to acknowledge 'the judge'. Firstly, it tricks us into thinking we have to be 'good' at writing before we've practised it. You wouldn't expect that of a baby learning to walk, or someone learning to play the trumpet, or how to drive a bus – writing also takes practice. Secondly, 'the judge' stops us from redrafting. Everyone writes rubbish first drafts, as Anne Lamott points out in *Bird by Bird* in an essay called 'Shitty First Drafts'. But if you listen to the judge, and don't realise that writing develops in the redrafting (again and again and again) – then you might give up before you have even got going.

The difference between freewriting and 'morning pages'

One interesting take on 'writing down what you are thinking' is Julia Cameron's 'morning pages'. The concept is explained in Cameron's books – for instance in *The Sound of Paper* (2006) – and on her website. The idea is that you write in a journal for three pages every morning before getting out of bed, that you get down all the mundane, trivial things in your head. You don't re-read your morning pages. They're a way of clearing out the clutter – and not for idea generation. You can hear Julia Cameron speak about morning pages in short video on her website. The URL is at the end of this chapter.

Try teaching someone else to be creative

Is it possible to teach someone to be creative? We'll come back to this idea later in the book. Occasionally I'll stop and ask you to teach a classmate part of your writing process. It's a way to reflect on what you do. This is, of course, optional. For now, simply have a quick go! You may or may not feel confident about it, but you already have a creative process; for instance, the way in which you come up with ideas. Can you explain it to someone else? Start to discover and to record your own unique process. Then explain that creative process to someone else, breaking it down for them so they can try out some of the techniques. That's a form of creative teaching.

Crucially, you're not saying (in a stern voice!) 'You must practise creatively in the same way I do, because there is no other way!' You're saying: 'Here's what worked for me. What works for you? Will any of these ideas help?'

For example, it wouldn't have occurred to me to go on a writing walk, specifically to think about my stories and characters, if another writer hadn't suggested it to me years ago. Now several of my ex-students go on writing walks because I suggested it to them. None of us invented walking, or writing walks, neither was there any coercion involved! The best kind of teaching is facilitation.

I've found one of the most successful ways to understand my own creative process is to try to explain it to someone else. Several other people have explained their creative processes too. Have a look at Mason Currey's *Daily Rituals* for examples.

When I suggest freewriting (and the other tools in the toolkit) in workshops it's because I broke down my own creative process and noticed what I did, then wanted to share that process with my students. As above, I wasn't meaning to say 'you must practise creatively in the same way I do, because there is no other way!' But rather 'Here's what worked for me. What works for you? Will any of these ideas help?' This book shares the same ethos.

Possibly because some of us are used to being 'taught to the test' at school, some workshop participants took this to mean that they 'had to' do freewriting even if they hated it! This disgruntlement applied to the other tools as well, but it was freewriting that often came in for the most ire, probably because it's used as a way into the other tools. If you're feeling like that, here is my answer: this week try teaching someone else to be creative using the method suggested above. See what happens and discuss the results.

Discussion

- What was easy / hard about freewriting?
- Have you ever done anything like it before? Where? When? Did it help?
- What does it mean to be creative?
- Can you *learn* to be creative? Can you *teach* creativity? How would you do it?
- Is creativity innate? Does everyone have it?
- Can you practise and get better at creativity? Or perhaps we need to unlearn the suppression of our creativity, as it were?

- Is creativity only ever unprompted / spur of the moment? Or is it always planned for, and carefully crafted?

If you want a full discussion of these questions, take a look at Rob Pope's 2005 book *Creativity*. I've written about it myself in a short essay called 'Searching for the Bandaged Place' that came out in a book called *The Creative Critic* in 2018. The references are at the end of this chapter.

Want more?

- Get hold of Anne Lamott's *Bird by Bird*. Read and discuss the essay called 'Shitty First Drafts.'
- Take a look at Dinty Moore's *The Mindful Writer*, and discuss what he says about inspiration in the section called 'The Writer's Mind.'

Summary of week three

Several writing practitioners tell us to try versions of this tool. It has various names. Peter Elbow calls it 'freewriting' (Elbow 1998: 13). Write what's in your head without thinking about it first. The rules are usually: don't edit as you go, don't think first, and keep going. Sometimes you do it for a set time, or there is a writing constraint added, such as writing in character. Don't confuse freewriting with the literary technique called 'stream of consciousness'.

You might use freewriting to: get past the judge (Brande, 1981: 56), as a warm up, as a form of idea generation or self-expression, for example. Julia Cameron's 'morning pages' aren't exactly the same as freewriting as you don't re-read your morning pages. They're a way of clearing out the clutter instead.

Can you write about your own creative process? Could you explain it to someone else? Is it possible to teach someone to be creative?

Works Cited

Brande, Dorothea. *Becoming a Writer*. Tarcher, 1981.

Cameron, Julia. *The Sound of Paper: Inspiration and Practical Guidance for Starting the Creative Process*. Penguin, 2006.

Cameron, Julia. *The Artist's Way: The Spiritual Path to Higher Creativity*. Pan, 1995. http://juliacameronlive.com/basic-tools/morning-pages/

Cope, Wendy. *Making Cocoa for Kingsley Amis*. Faber, 1986.

Currey, Mason. *Daily Rituals: How Great Minds Make Time, Find Inspiration, and Get to Work*. 2013.

Elbow, Peter. *Writing with Power: Techniques for Mastering the Writing Process*. Oxford University Press, 1998.

Goldberg, Natalie. *Writing Down the Bones: Freeing the Writer Within*. Shambhala, 1986.

Joyce, James. *Ulysses*. Penguin Modern Classics, 2000.

Lamott, Anne. *Bird by Bird: Instructions on Writing and Life*. Bantam, 1995.

Moore, Dinty. *The Mindful Writer* Wisdom Publications, 2012.

Tondeur, Louise. 'Searching for 'the bandaged place''. In Emily Orley and Katja Hilevaara. *The Creative Critic: writing as / about practice*. Routledge, 2018.

Pope, Rob. *Creativity: Theory, History, Practice*. Routledge, 2005.

Woolf, Virginia. *Mrs Dalloway*. Penguin, 2000.

Weeks Four: Close Observation

What's included in this chapter?

The next two tools are Close Observation and Creative Visualisation. Although both tools sound visually biased, actually Close Observation and Creative Visualisation employ any or all of the senses.

These chapters mainly consists of essays I have written over the years on Close Observation and Creative Visualisation, discussion of the role they have played in my writing life, and the exercises I have used myself and in workshops I have facilitated.

Week Four is about Close Observation, a powerful, meditative technique that can really help you to add detail and atmosphere to your writing.

Try this exercise

- Find a mundane, everyday object. Observe the

object for five minutes. After the observation, write what you experienced.
- Next try imagining a mundane, everyday object in your mind's eye. Imagine using it. Fill in the detail. Write about it.
- Now look back over what you've written. Underline any phrases or images that you particularly like.

Watching the nettles

I first went to Arvon when I was nineteen. I was the end of my first year as a (very shy) undergraduate studying Drama at UEA and was given a grant to attend, without which I wouldn't have been able to afford to go. It was a *Starting to Write* course at Totleigh Barton in Devon. I was the youngest on the course and was very nervous about sharing my work. I had only just begun to write prose at that stage, as I grew up writing poetry, although I did attempt my first novel when I was fourteen on an old typewriter. (I still have it in a folder somewhere!)

The workshop activity I remember the most clearly was the observation exercise we did. We had to go and look at something for forty-five minutes and then report back. I watched a patch of nettles. When we went back inside, a small piece of paper told us: *It starts to move*. That was the writing prompt.

What occurred during that activity was one of the most exciting things that had ever happened to me as a writer. There was something transformational about that activity which meant that I would never look at things in the same way again. I went away and wrote a ghost story about a body in the nettles and frightened myself, sitting until late into the night at the long table in the medieval dining room, with the creaks and groans of the house going on around me.

The other thing I remember clearly was the trifle I made when it was our turn to cook. I was SO proud of it! It may be many years ago, but I can still recall the looks on people's faces as I carried it in. There is something about cooking and writing that go together for me. I find them equally tactile and earthy – I like the feeling of getting my hands covered in ink (or mango juice).

I have been on two retreats since my Totleigh course, and have visited all of the centres. At Moniack Mhor, while it was still part of Arvon, I wrote a substantial part of my second novel. The feeling of peace and creativity is something you can reach out and touch there, like magic.

When I taught my first course for Arvon, I was up at Lumb Bank with Ann Redmon. We were doing *Starting to Write the Novel*. I asked the students to try the observation exercise I did down in Devon and when I kicked it off I told them then that I felt I had been full circle.

Although I eventually did one of the best known creative writing courses in the UK, I had never been a creative writing course type of person. I was much more likely to write pages and pages in secret and stuff it in a drawer! Arvon was different for me. It brought me out of myself and gave me a space in which to write at a time when I was young and inexperienced and when I really needed the encouragement to continue.

Probably because of my upbringing and the way in which that particular brand of evangelical Christianity was not accepting of my sexuality, and knocked my confidence, I didn't know whether I could write effectively until much later. But it was Arvon that set me off on the journey. My first two novels are about transformational places too. People sometimes ask me why I write and I have to tell them that it is an obsession – and it is always close observation of place that I come back to.

It was while I was at Lumb Bank that I found out that Julia Darling had died. Julia wrote a quotation for the front of my first novel, *The Water's Edge*, and sent me a little card for the launch which gave me a moment of peace amongst all the mayhem. She was very kind to me when I went to visit her and her family in Newcastle. Julia was one of my encouragers, one of the women writers who went before me, showing me the way through all the madness and topsy-turvy-ness of being a writer or any kind of creator.

When I got to Lumb, there was a photo of Julia Darling with Jackie Kay in the room I was staying in, in fact there were photos of writers all over the house, and I was reminded again that writers and teachers go before us, showing us the way and I know that Arvon helped Ann and me to inspire new writers in the way that my teachers inspired me.

When I found out what had happened, I discovered a poem Julia had written called 'How To Deal With Terrible News' – in other words she was still teaching me. I love her book *The Poetry Cure*, which she edited with Cynthia Fuller and, although it's hard to find now, I recommend it to anyone who has ever been through the experience of being ill or interacting with health services.

In the spirit of passing the baton, try the nettle activity. One day soon or a long time in the future I hope you'll teach it to another writer.

As this is a Small Steps Guide, let's move on now and look at how we can apply the Small Steps Method to the writing process. Why? To help us to get better at self-reflection. (By the way, you could class the above description of my time at Arvon as a personal reflective essay, in case you need an example.)

Breaking it down

How do we nail down that elusive term 'creativity'? As I've said before, I decided to look at my own creative process and come up with a list of what I actually did. Lists are good, by the way, because they free you from having to write in sentences and they promote a kind of word association that becomes easier with space around the words. That was the start of a journey that eventually led to this book.

Think back to the last time you practised, or think more broadly about how you are creative in your everyday life, and see if you can come up with a list of the steps you followed. You might have already done this during Week Three on freewriting. If so, dig out that list now.

Green Machine

Try this exercise called *Green Machine*. It's an opportunity to be creative and later, if you want to, you can take apart the creative process and see how it works. This exercise focuses on the colour green. Substitute a different colour if that doesn't work for you, and if you can't get outside, observe through a window or a door.

- Go for a walk. Notice the different versions of the colour green you see along the way.
- When you get home, close your eyes and think about your walk. Imagine all the detail you can. Picture the colours.
- Go through all of your senses one by one and recall the experience.
- Now think specifically about the different versions of the colour green you saw.

In a notebook make a list of the kinds of green you saw by pairing 'green' with a noun. These don't have to make sense. Simply generate pairs of words, letting go of the idea of logical sounding phrases for now. For example, 'mud-green', 'fire-green', 'bus-green', 'school-green', 'book-green', 'gravestone-green'. The idea here is to get round your internal censor and have fun.

- Once you've generated a list of paired words, circle those you like.
- Edit your list. This time, try to describe, as specifically as you can, the kind of green you saw. You are trying to 'make sense' at this point but the sense you make could be surprising or unusual.
- Play a word association game with yourself, using any of your paired words. Generate another list.

You can take this in any direction: a poem called 'Green', the beginning of a a sci-fi novel set on an emerald covered planet, a feature article about local park upkeep, an interview with an older person about what your local environment looked like when they were a child, a piece of life writing about significant natural places.

Once you have tried the Green Machine exercise, or thought about the last time you practised, write down what you did. Don't analyse too much. Make a list of *what you actually did*. Anything is allowed. For example:

- Moved
- Used all of my senses
- Thought in pictures
- Observed the world around me

Then describe each as a process or as a creative tool.

Creative Writing students are often asked to 'reflect on the process,' but how do you do it? We're learning how reflection works by analysing the 'green machine' activity more than we would in the usual run of things! Here's what I did when I worked on the 'green machine' activity. What about you?

I used:

- Freewriting, meaning I wrote without stopping and without editing.
- A combination of Close Observation and Live Writing. I went on a walk to observe the environment.
- My senses. I observed my locality with 'writer's eyes' and experienced the world around me.
- Creative Visualisation. I pictures details of the walk when I came home.

Making it easy

Psychologists have proved that the easier a task becomes, the more likely we are to do it. This may seem obvious when reduced to a single sentence but consider the implications: make stopping smoking or road safety or recycling seem 'easy' and our brains get hoodwinked into making life a little bit better! This is also a principle we can apply to learning and teaching creativity.

'Be creative' does not sound easy. It sounds abstract, and possibly elitist, too; something 'other people' have time for. It might sound 'childish' to you, suggesting that to be creative we need to get back to being more child-like and more playful. Of course, difficult isn't necessarily bad – it can be extremely productive. More on that in a moment.

But if you're having trouble accessing your creativity, you can 'make it easy' by breaking it down into small steps like this. For instance:

- Find a stone.
- Hold it in your hand.
- Feel its weight.
- What colour is it?
- Is the surface rough or smooth?
- What does it smell like?
- Describe the place you found the stone.
- Who might use the stone? What for? Where has it been?
- Someone *remembers* using the stone. Write down the memory.

As before, you can take this in any direction: a poem about textures and smells, a murder mystery that starts on a beach, a feature article about unemployment in tourist resorts, an interview with an older person about their memories of childhood holidays, a piece of life writing based on memories of your own, triggered by the stone.

Why it isn't easy

Facilitating the process and making it as easy as possible to be creative in the first place is important. But at the same time one of the most important aspects of creativity is that it isn't easy. In other words, don't take the easiest route while writing, because:

1. You have to look in a new way. It's sometimes easy to go for the most obvious: the stereotyped phrase, story, character, image, or situation, the

one we've seen repeated on TV or online / on social. Creativity means avoiding the most obvious path or reworking it. We're not finding something completely new, but often we're looking at ordinary, mundane things in a new way. This is known as defamiliarisation and comes from the work of Viktor Shklovsky.

2. You have to be brave. When everyone else seems to be going for an uninteresting approach or the same-old thing, it takes some nerve to stand out from the crowd, to say 'yes, I am creative,' to get your idea out, especially as it might be criticised. Contemporary writer and speaker Brené Brown calls this being 'in the arena'.

3. You have to be committed. Creative practice takes practice. There is no such thing as getting it right first time, or even getting it right. With a media (seemingly) full of instant gratification, it can be hard to understand that creativity is not about instant results or bolts of lightning from the blue. The more you practise, the better at it you get. As Scottish climber William Hutchison Murray put it 'until one is committed, there is hesitancy, the chance to draw back, always ineffectiveness…'

Why constraint is important

One of the things I discovered as I looked at my own creative processes was that anything at all can be an idea (or perhaps it's better to say anything can be a starting point or a trigger or can tell a story). In a way, creativity is a way of describing *your ability to shape something*, like a potter shapes clay. That is, we take the material (the idea, starting point or trigger) and we apply a constraint to it. This can be as simple as playing a Creative Writing game or as complicated as plotting a 100,000-word novel. There is something about the constraint that allows one to be creative.

Making the steps small enough

You've looked at your own creative processes and have begun to write down what you do when you're 'being creative'. Extend and develop your list over the coming weeks, remembering the different approaches you took and recording them in a notebook. Once your list is fairly substantial, turn what you have into a list of short writing exercises. If you're in a workshop group, you might like to have a go at teaching them to someone else.

Take steps backwards until you have a set of instructions. Make the first instruction is as simple as possible. How do you make sure your steps are small enough? Keep taking steps back until you can't simplify the process any more. Look at my close observation exercise called 'Find a Stone' above for an example.

A final word about Close Observation

As well as deliberately examining something closely, Close Observation is also about noticing the detail in your everyday life. In fact, Susan Sontag calls writers 'professional observers […] of the world' (Sontag 2011). Awareness and sensitivity are vital. As writers, we have particular uses for close observation of objects, places and people, and for specificity and detail, because we need to describe the world in new and unusual ways for our readers.

Close observation is also about travelling through life with a writer's eyes: keeping awake, observing the world as you experience it, noticing things, telling your own story, thinking about the story behind the dropped cigarette or the lines on a face. Notice your local area, the way the bins look, the front doors, the street, the fields, the trees and other natural objects.

Discussion

- What do you notice about carrying the notebook around? What effect does it have?
- Have you used Close Observation before?
- Do you find it useful?
- Discuss the 'Green Machine' activity.
- What do you think about the idea that 'turning up' is more important than inspiration?

Want more?

Take a look at *The Sound of Paper* by Julia Cameron and *The Five-Minute Writer* by Margret Geraghty and discuss them.

Read the William Hutchison Murray quotation below and discuss whether you agree. You can find a fuller version of this quotation on Murray's Wikipedia page:

'Until one is committed, there is hesitancy, the chance to draw back, always ineffectiveness […] that the moment one definitely commits oneself, then […] all sorts of things occur to help one that would never otherwise have occurred.'

Summary of week four

When I first went to the Arvon Foundation, aged 19, the tutors set an activity that changed my life: I watched a patch of nettles for 45 minutes. It taught me about the role of the writer as observer, and about the importance of looking for specificity and detail. Close observation is also about travelling through life with writer's eyes: keeping awake, observing the world around you.

When I looked at my own creative process and came up with a list of what I actually did, I noticed that I was looking closely at the specificity and detail in the world around me, and that walks were highly productive.

I also discovered that I was most creative when I looked at the world in a new way, when I was brave enough to stand out from the crowd, and when I practised (over and over). I realised that a constraint or a rule is enabling, although it sometimes feels like it might not be! Breaking the process down into small steps helps with the sense of overwhelm.

Works Cited

Brown, Brené. *Daring Greatly*. Penguin, 2013.

Cameron, Julia. *The Sound of Paper: Inspiration and Practical Guidance for Starting the Creative Process*. Penguin, 2006.

Darling, Julia and Cynthia Fuller, eds. *The Poetry Cure*. Bloodaxe, 2005. See: http://juliadarling.co.uk/works/poetry/the-poetry-cure/

Darling, Julia. 'How to Deal With Terrible News.' In *Indelible, Miraculous*. Arc Publications, 2015. Available at: https://www.theguardian.com/books/2005/jan/05/poetry [Accessed September 2017]

Geraghty, Margret. *The Five-Minute Writer*. How to Books, 2009.

Murray, William. *The Scottish Himalayan Expedition*. J.M. Dent & Sons, 1951.

Shklovsky, Viktor. *Viktor Shklovsky: A Reader.* Bloomsbury, 2016.

Sontag, Susan. 'From the 48th Congress of International PEN: Citizens of Language'. *PEN America: A Journal for Writers and Readers.* Issue 14. New York: PEN America. 2011. Pp. 99- 100. Print.

Tondeur, Louise. *The Water's Edge*. Review, 2003.

Week Five: Creative Visualisation

An introduction to Creative Visualisation

Here I describe how you could use Creative Visualisation in a workshop, or how individuals can use it to enhance their practice. I start by explaining visualisation and then give three levels of exercises: short, extended and whole group. Of course, all of these can be adapted and can be tackled in a simple or complex way.

Approach each activity in two stages: the visualisation stage, followed by writing in a notebook, either with a constraint applied or by simply recording impressions.

As before, if you find visualisation hard, then discover your own alternative. Start by writing about each or any of the senses.

What is Creative Visualisation?

Visualisation means actively experiencing something in your mind, using all the senses you have available to you. Visualisation is a skill many of us use in everyday activities.

For instance, it might happen when you daydreams, have an idea or a brainwave, remember something that has happened, or look forward to an occasion in the future. Although there tends to be a visual bias, the name visualisation is misleading because the technique is not only about seeing a *picture* in your mind, but rather about *experiencing* something with your mind.

Creative Visualisation is the same as visualisation but it is more deliberate. You might, for instance, deliberately experience going to a relaxing place in your mind in order to unwind, or to help you sleep. Coaches might encourage us to imagine ourselves succeeding before an interview or an important event, or to imagine ourselves in five years time.

You might listen to someone reading a guided visualisation, either live or on audio, in order to meditate. Once you get used to them, these mental experiences are sustained over a period of time and hence often likened to a journey.

Remember that Creative Visualisation is not only about *seeing* a picture in your mind. The emphasis is on all of the senses you have available to you. In a guided visualisation you'll be encouraged to see, taste, smell, touch or hear the environment you are imagining. You'll also be encouraged to fill in the small unusual details and to create a sense of atmosphere.

Why use Creative Visualisation as a writer?

You might imagine a journey or a house or a place or a person for to write about. If you visualise what it would be like to be a character from your story, Creative Visualisation can also feel a little like method acting!

Using Creative Visualisation enables us to get our

minds into a state in which we are more able to access our creativity. This is sometimes described by practitioners as *bypassing the conscious mind*, which one can take to mean *bypassing the inner critic*.

In sum, a writer might use Creative Visualisation to:

- imagine a character in an environment
- experience the world whilst standing in the shoes of a character
- imagine a place in our writing. This could be a chair in which a character sits, a room, a house or a whole town.

Creative Visualisation can help with imagery too. For instance, based on a visualisation, write about a man falling out of bed. Close your eyes and go through all of the senses you have available to you, asking yourself: what would I experience if I were in this environment? What can I taste? What can I touch? What can I hear? Then write down some images about falling.

Short exercises to try

It can help start with short exercises to get used to the technique. Here are some simple ones – pick one or two. Practise for ten minutes before writing a description in your notebook.

- Imagine standing at a window and seeing a rainbow.
- Imagine lighting a candle and watching the flame.
- Picture yourself standing in front of a fireplace.
- Think of a time you experienced fireworks.

- Listen to Mozart. What shapes can you see?
- In your imagination, stand under a waterfall. Let the water rush past and concentrate on the sound.
- Let your mind take you on an adventure: Climb a mountain or queue up for a roller coaster.
- Imagine the sense of touch and apply it to a fictional character. For instance, imagine a ninety-year-old woman. What it is like to hold her hand? What it is like to touch her face?
- Think about the first time you or a character experienced snow.

Creative Visualisation and the world around you.

Nature provides a rich source of images for visualisation, some of which are used in the practical ideas above. Here are ten more suggestions, but also, try to be aware of the world around you when you are outside and store up your own experiences to use in your visualisations. Top tip: do not try all of these in one day, you will overload your brain – space them out over the coming months!

1. Think about the complexity of a tree trunk – old, gnarled, full of secrets, full of life, strong, weathered by experience.
2. Imagine you are holding a leaf. Experience every detail. What does it feel like in your hand? Imagine you are next to a big tree. What can you hear?
3. Imagine the face of a sunflower. Can you note all the details?
4. Focus on a colour from nature. The red of a poppy. The yellow of a field of mustard. The

changing colour of the sea, from blue to green to grey. The orange, yellow and purple of a fire.
5. Imagine you are near a mountain. How big is it? Are there trees climbing up the side? Do you see snow or clouds at the top?
6. You are sitting on the shore near to where the waves are breaking. Listen to the sound they make.
7. Think of the image of the earth seen from space. Imagine you are actually seeing the world from this unique point of view as a human being. Now imagine you were visiting the planet for the first time, how would you feel?
8. Remember a storm you once experienced and how powerful it was. Think about the colours, the feeling of strength, the lightening, the wind and rain.
9. Hands can perform so many different tasks: picking up a pen, throwing and catching a ball, typing, holding someone else's hand. Think about your own hands.
10. Imagine a dancer or remember a dance you have watched or taken part in. Think about the movements the human body can make.

Developing your skills

Creative Visualisation encourages the use of the senses in particular. We are then able to apply what we have learnt to our writing, asking what can I, or my characters, see, taste, smell, touch or feel, and hear?

The five suggestions that follow focus on the senses individually, but are also intended to help you create a whole picture using all of your senses. If you do not have the use of one or more of your senses, then focus on the other activities. I suggest that you practise the Creative Visualisation for half an hour (build up to it) and then write a description in your notebook.

Sound

We are surrounded by sound all the time. Language, sounds from nature, sounds of the city, the washing machine spinning, post dropping through the letterbox, the television, water running, or our favourite music.

Our brains are able to process and distinguish between an amazing number of different nuances of sound. Think of the skill involved in recognising a piece of music, noticing the sadness in someone's voice, or in knowing who's approaching from the sound of their footsteps. Sounds can be a source of joy, but too much creates a stressful overload.

What feelings do these sounds create for you?

- water lapping by the side of a lake
- a cuckoo calling
- the wind in the trees
- a storm and the sound of rain on the roof
- the sound of drums playing

Choose some different types of music to play. Close your eyes and watch the pictures each creates in your mind.

Smell

Smells are very powerful. They can trigger a memory of a place or person we thought we had forgotten years ago. We often forget to include them in our writing, but a smell can evoke a place succinctly for your reader. What feelings do these smells create for you?

- Freshly baked bread,
- disinfectant,
- lavender,
- bonfire smoke,
- old books,
- leather,
- cut grass,
- sage and onion stuffing,
- pine needles,
- rain,
- mashed potato,
- clean towels.

Try out different smells around your home: coffee, paper, the dirty clothes basket, clean washing, shower gel. What does each evoke? Make a list of words.

Sight

We are bombarded with picture messages all the time. Flick through a magazine, turn on the TV, look up at an advertising hoarding and you'll see pictures being used to create an emotional response, to beguile us, tempt or challenge us, turn us on, inspire us, or make us laugh. Sometimes the juxtaposition of images in a photograph or painting can make us see the world in a different way.

Is there a photo you have seen which inspires you in this way? Try to find an interesting picture to use by doing some research. Share it with others.

Focus on the photograph. See all the detail, the light and shade, the colour. What happened just before this photo was taken? Just after? What feelings are created? Recreate the scene in your mind.

How often do you really look at the things around you? In your home, look at a familiar object. Why is it designed in the way it is? Look for the details. Next time you go outside, really look at the things you pass. Later recreate the scene in your mind.

Taste

Sometimes we can eat food in such a rush that we forget how fantastic good tasting food can be. Food is actually better for you if you take time to prepare, eat and enjoy it because your digestion will improve and this enables us to think about what we are putting into our bodies. Trying foods from different cultures can wake up and challenge our sense of taste.

Decide which tastes you love and which you hate. Try to add more tastes to the list of those you love every day for a week. Try to recreate your favourite taste in your mouth.

Eat or drink something that you find both delicious and empowering. Think carefully about the taste as you experience it. Practise savouring it. Perhaps you could try some contrasting tastes, such as honey and lemon, or cheese and apple. Now write down a description of the taste. If you are working in a group, you could share experiences. In one of my workshops years ago, a student brought in some hot chocolate for participants to try and then write about.

Touch

Perhaps this is the most intimate of the senses, and it is also one of contrasts. Touch can be compassionate or violent, soft or hard, gentle or forceful, rough or smooth. There are many visualisations you can practise where you are holding, touching and experiencing an object or an environment. For example, you can try imaging the touch of grass, sand or paving stones beneath your feet. Here are some more:

- Think of the feeling you get when you sink into a hot bubble bath.
- Imagine what it's like to float in a swimming pool on a sunny day.
- Imagine swimming in the sea in the rain.
- Find an object. Touch it carefully, and decide why it is interesting to you. Close your eyes and touch your object again. Share experiences with other participants if you are working in a group.

Mini-scripts for tutors to read out

1. You are in comfortable surroundings: decide where you are and imagine it in your mind. Perhaps you are on holiday lying on a beautiful sandy beach, sitting having a picnic with friends, or in your room at home. You can hear a wonderful sound. Perhaps it is music playing, or the sound of water, or animals. Listen to the sound carefully. Let it fill your mind. Gradually it begins to fade.

2. Imagine standing by a window. You can see a blue harbour full of boats. What does the air smell like? Feel the sea breeze on your face. Imagine the scene in your mind. Imagine the smell of the sea.
3. Picture your own imaginary scene from a window – is it a relaxing scene, a canal-side or a field or the view of a beautiful lake? Or is it a scene of hustle and bustle – a market place, a street café, a lively carnival or city scene? Imagine the colours. Look for the detail.
4. You are in a comfortable place. Imagine your surroundings. You have something to eat or drink in your hand. Something wonderful. Something life giving. When you take a bite or a sip you can feel it nourishing your body. Imagine the wonderful taste.
5. Imagine you are on a pebble beach. You pick up a pebble and now you are holding it in your hand. What is the surface of the pebble like? Is it hot or cold? Is it rough or smooth? How heavy is it? Are there ridges or holes? Is it flat or round or pointed? What does it feel like?

Extending visualisations for groups

Often used in a group situation, guided visualisation takes your mind on a journey, so that you can experience where it leads you. Participants do not know before the work where the journey will lead.

The following extended visualisations are intended for a facilitator to use with a group, during a Creative Writing session. Make notes in your notebook afterwards. When you are leading an extended visualisation, take your time, be a storyteller and think about the quality of your voice. Remember to breathe. Leave pauses after each new idea and adapt the visualisation to the needs of those in the group.

These 'journeys' can be turned into pieces of drama or stories or poems. For instance, after completing the visualisation once, the facilitator goes back to the beginning and repeats the story allowing time for participants to write about in their own specific journeys.

1. Imagine you are in your favourite place. You feel very comfortable and secure. Where are you sitting / lying / standing? What can you see, smell, hear, taste, and touch? Think of the colours. Think of the details. What objects are there? Are there any other people there? Why is it your favourite place? (This can be the starting place for many visualisations – especially where participants imagine they are going on a journey – as this provides a safe space to set out from and return to and also provides somewhere to examine what has been found on the way or the experience of the journey itself.)
2. Think of a building. What is the outside of the building like? Imagine the rooms. Visit each one in turn. Feel the floor under your feet. What sensations does it arouse? Explore the building. Let light play through the windows; watch the wind playing with the curtains. Walk around the outside of the building. What does the air taste like?
3. You are walking along the bank of a river. Imagine what you can see and hear. Can you hear the flow of the river? What does the air

smell like? If the place had a taste what would it taste like? Imagine you are reaching out and touching something – the ground, the bark of a tree, a rock – what does it feel like? Walk along the bank of the river and imagine the scenery begins to change – what does it look like now? Perhaps you have moved from a grassy bank to rock or sand. Use all the senses you have available to you as before. What does it look like, sound like, feel like, taste like, smell like?

Discussion

- How do you feel when you practise Creative Visualisation? Challenged, uncomfortable, peaceful, enthusiastic, sleepy?
- How do you think you'll use Creative Visualisation in your writing life?
- Does Creative Visualisation come easily to you or do you find it difficult? What could you do instead?

Want more?

Try the Guided Meditations on the Meditainment website at https://www.meditainment.com. This is a paid service, but you can get started for free.

Summary of week five

This week we've looked at what Creative Visualisation is and how to use it to enhance your writing. We've gone through each of the senses one at a time and discovered how sensory detail can bring a piece of writing alive for our readers.

Visualisation means actively experiencing something in your mind, using all the senses you have available to you. Creative Visualisation is the same as visualisation but it is more deliberate, often involving a journey. You might deliberately experience going to a relaxing place in your mind in order to unwind, for instance. A writer might use Creative Visualisation to imagine a character in an environment or to experience the world from a character's point of view. You've also experienced a set of extended group visualisations that you can try in workshops.

Week Six: Writing Props

Writing Prompts

'Writing prompts' is a generic term for starting points, or anything we use to kick off a piece of writing. It's likely you're familiar with this concept already. You can find writing prompts in books, on Twitter, in writing magazines and in teaching resources, for example.

I've seen erroneous text messages and computer games used as prompts. Really, any stimulus could be a writing prompt if you say it is, but there will be something different or thought-provoking about a good one, because they're supposed to generate ideas or to inspire you to write.

Now for something slightly different

In my working life, I started out as a drama teacher, so when I think of a 'workshop' I go to a drama workshop in my head, and when I think of prompts or starting points, I go to the prop box and the costume cupboard or the interesting masks we once got to play with when I was a drama student!

So, while written instructions or a flat image on a page are often useful (my first novel started like that) this tool is about actual objects. The term 'props' comes with its own contexts to do with theatre and playwriting, but for our purposes we're going to use it to mean an actual object or group of objects that's used as a starting point for a piece of writing.

The other tools we've covered involve writing props to a certain extent: observing or visualising objects, for example, and freewriting about them.

How to use writing props

There are two main methods here. The first one involves a found object. In workshops I usually suggest using a found object from nature, but it doesn't have to be natural. By the way, if you can't take your found object back to the workshop or back home with you, note down what it was or take a photo of it, or write in front of it.

The second involves setting up a prop or set of props in front of the workshop group (or yourself if you're working alone), and noticing the divergent ideas it generates. Props I've used with workshop groups include:

- a suitcase full of props to depict a character. I often add sound effects to this one to suggest it's been found on a beach and set it up in advance of the workshop so students can examine it as they arrive.
- a pair of wellies. I have a lovely pair of rainbow coloured boots that I used to take camping with

me. These work well as they are unusual looking and on the scruffy side.
- a bin bag, full of props rather than actual rubbish.
- a wooden spoon, with no explanation.
- a tableaux of objects in a spotlight, like a scene on stage without people, that's set up before students enter the space. An open umbrella works well in this set up as it helps to demarcate the stage space, and suggests specific symbolisms.

For more prop-based starting points, see part four of my book *Drama Lesson Plans for Busy Teachers: Book One*.

Objects tell a story or suggest images

Why use objects? Because objects are part of your life. Even if only for the length of the writing workshop you are in, you have encountered those objects up close. The object's timeline has crossed with yours. I received a gift of a rocking chair that belonged to my Great-Grandmother and it's sitting next to me in my writing shed as I type this. Not a picture of it, a real tactile, imperfect object that I encounter every day. I never met my Great-Grandmother, but now the object she bought and cherished is in my timeline too.

The object, whatever it is, tells a story. Who used it? Who made it? Where did they live? What family did they have? What materials were used to make the object? And where are they from? You could project this narrative into the future too, and it doesn't have to be life writing or nonfiction; you could fictionalise a story about an object.

When you have the thing in front of you, this technique is so much more powerful.

You will have noticed that the tools in the toolkit intersect with one another. The obvious link here is with Close Observation. Find an object and observe it closely – keep going past boredom until you start seeing something interesting – and note down what you observe. Try to find unusual images and ways of describing the object so that the reader sees it in a new way.

Objects tell us about ourselves

I sometimes send students out of the room to find objects, which they bring back into the workshop after the break. Once a student found a huge chunk of tree that had been sawn off quite near the stump. He carried it up the stairs on his shoulders and threw it (not entirely on purpose, it was heavy) onto the floor near to where I was standing. I think this was in part a performance, and in part a comment on what he thought of the writing exercise.

Sometimes beginner writers think they've got an exercise 'wrong' when they've actually got it absolutely right. Of course I didn't want anyone to hurt themselves carrying large pieces of wood up the stairs, but he had found an interesting object which is what I asked for. His response said something about the way in which some students learn to respond to creative teaching, but it wasn't 'wrong'. A chunk of tree still works as an object, as long as you approach the writing itself with authenticity. (If you're running a workshop, you may wish to stipulate a maximum size or easy carry-ability!)

More common is this response, also not 'wrong': when students forget to find an object during the break and use the cup of coffee they bought, or a cigarette lighter, or a biro from the bottom of their bag. Again, observing these objects still works. They still tell a story. They make you think about throwaway things you don't usually notice.

Basic Props Exercises

- Find an object in the room you are in now and tell its story.
- Collect some props together. Put them in a suitcase or a bag or even a wastepaper bin.
- Go out for a walk and collect or photograph some 'found objects'.
- If possible, visit a junk shop or two.
- Look out for and collect ephemera, such as bus tickets, postcards, receipts and shopping lists.

The Bag

Here is a props exercise that takes things a bit further. This activity involves Close Observation, Creative Visualisation and Freewriting. If you don't have a real bag, brainstorm types of bag (you can fill a whole whiteboard, believe me!) and then pick one to use for the activity and visualise it in a particular environment.

1. Find a bag – any kind of bag will do – a carrier, a shopping bag, a lunchbox, a body bag, a suitcase, a briefcase, a school bag, a sports bag – and fill it with random objects. These can be everyday objects, or whatever you choose. For an extra twist, ask a friend, or your classmates, to fill the bag for you.
2. Decide on an environment – a beach, a

mountain, a train station, a shopping centre, an airport – anywhere will do. Close your eyes and visualise it very clearly. Fill in all the details using all of your senses. Or simply describe the environment using the senses. This is the environment where the bag has been found. It has been left behind by an (imaginary, fictitious) character.
3. Tip the bag out in front of you and examine the contents carefully. Why has the bag been left behind? What did these things mean to the character? What can you tell about him / her from the contents of the bag? Where is he / she now?
4. Write from the point of view of either the person who left the bag behind OR from the point of view of three people in the person's life, switching from character to character. Use either first or third person.

I've given you some examples below, so you can see what I mean, but a memorable take on this exercise came from two students in the same drama class, one who decided his bag was a lunchbox, containing prawn sandwiches, found on the steps of a psychiatric hospital, the other who decided her bag was a bin bag, stuffed full of money, found in a children's sandpit.

I mentioned above that in one writing workshop I used a suitcase full of props with sound effects playing in the background. That was also a version of the bag exercise, although I stipulated the kind of bag and the environment upfront. One student based the novel he wrote for NaNoWriMo on that workshop – my favourite example of using writing props to tell a story.

By the way, I have done this activity many times with many different kinds of groups and if you brainstorm types of bag on the whiteboard, someone always says 'body bag' – good suggestion – someone else will say 'old bag,' and usually, after sniggering, someone at the back will suggest 'ball bag.' (I usually pretend to be oblivious to the double-meaning of this 'joke'.)

Having a real bag as an example helps, so does getting participants to brainstorm in pairs first, but I simply write all suggestions up on the whiteboard with no comment, apart from discounting 'old bag' because it's a tired, sexist metaphor and therefore won't work. Then I let the rules of the exercise take care of the rest. The outliers soon discover that it's actually more fun to engage with the activity than to be cynical or rude. On other occasions I've simply told them what people always tend to say before we start.

Examples

What kind of bag is it?

- Example 1: A bin bag
- Example 2: A suitcase

What objects are found in the bag?

- Example 1: bundles of £50 notes
- Example 2: a necklace, a passport, a scrap of paper with a phone number and a train ticket

Where is it found?

- Example 1: outside a church

- Example 2: washed up on a beach

The Drawer

Instead of using a bag full of objects, you can use a drawer. Try this. Reach into a drawer and pull out a random object. Repeat several times. Either:

- Write in character and respond to each item you pull it out as if it belonged to a fictional person.
- Or: make a list of what you find. Observe and then describe each object in detail.

Discussion

Talk about 'the bag' activity. What was challenging about it? What did you enjoy? Will you continue with the piece of writing you produced? Do you regularly use writing prompts? Do you like / dislike starting with a prop or group of props?

Want more?

Staying Alive, a Bloodaxe poetry collection, includes two poems about bags, one of them by Maura Dooley the other by Ruth Fainlight, that you might like to look up.

Summary of week six

While a 'writing prompt' is a generic term for anything that can kick off a piece of writing, we're using writing props, that is, actual objects. There's some crossover with the way you might use them in the theatre. Either go out and look for objects, and surprise yourself, or deliberately find a suggestive object at home, like a pair of boots, a bag or a suitcase.

Objects tell a story; you are witnessing them at one point in their timeline, but what else has happened to them and where did they come from? Objects suggest images. Objects tell us something about ourselves. If you would like to try an extended writing activity, fill a bag and write about it, or use a drawer to do similar. One of my workshop participants wrote a whole novel based on the bag activity.

Works Cited

Astley, Neil, ed. *Staying Alive: Real Poems for Unreal Times*. Bloodaxe. New ed, 2016, pp. 108-109.

Tondeur, Louise. *Drama Lesson Plans for Busy Teachers: 40 Ideas for drama that will bring the curriculum to life.* Suitcase Kids, 2017.

Week Seven: Live Writing

Live Writing

This technique involves a writer going to a particular place (a building, a park, or a museum for instance) and writing there and then about the space they are in. It could also be called 'total immersion writing' or 'writing in situ'. If you are writing for the stage, you might end up with what's called a 'site-specific performance'.

Live Writing uses close observation – because you write the specifics of what you see in front of you – and this is the most important skill you can use while doing it. It also uses Creative Visualisation because you visualise events happening in the space. It usually involves freewriting in a notebook: you record your impressions and type up a second draft later, editing as you go.

Of course places can be writing prompts and might well inspire a story, and will involve their own significant objects, but Live Writing encompasses more than that: as well as being inspired by the place, you also observe the minute details. Being there for a few hours (or a whole day) allows you to do so.

Live Writing Journeys

Another kind of Live Writing involves some kind of walk or journey. You might want to try it on a long train journey, for instance. Several of my students have been on writing walks, when they record their sense impressions as they go, sitting down when there is a bench available to write what they observe. They have also incorporated information about the locality (as a kind of contextual marginalia), poetry and prose, sketches and photographs. Graveyards, beaches and other liminal places are great for this kind of journey.

Once you've finished the journey and the writing / creating, you need to make an important decision about how the work will be presented. Often, if not always, these pieces are *about* walking, travelling and journeying, or being away from home. We'll talk more about journeys later in the book.

Live Writing as a performance

I've seen a rather more extroverted form of Live Writing, where the writer sits on a stage and writes live in front of an audience. Rest assured, that's not what I'm talking about here!

How I did it

I wrote a whole series of short stories by visiting places and writing while I was there. I did this long hand in notebooks. I edited later on a computer. Most of the venues were in London, where I lived at the time. I deliberately chose hidden out-of-the-way places that the general public might not have heard about. You can read more about the process on my website.

I made it a rule that the place had to be free to get into, there had to be somewhere to sit and write, and there had to be an indoors bit in case it rained, and a café in case of need for tea! I only deviated from these rules once. (Make up your own rules.) The short story collection that resulted is called *Unusual Places* and was published by Cultured Llama in 2018.

Take care of yourself

As you can see from the above, I made sure I could get tea and shelter from the rain. These things are important. I once had an enthusiastic student who went out in the middle of the night to do the following exercise. She was an adult, so it was her choice, but I advise against doing anything that could put you at risk.

If you want to write about somewhere a bit edgy, get *inspired* by the place, but think twice before doing writing in situ. And take it from me, if you're doing Live Writing in the UK, take a jumper and plan where you're going to shelter from the rain!

First Live Writing Exercise

You'll need a notebook, a pen and somewhere to write. This takes about forty minutes. Do it somewhere near to where you live.

1. Go outside and find somewhere to sit with your

notebook where you won't be disturbed. (If it's raining, a café with a view is fine!)
2. Immerse yourself in the place, using all your senses.
3. Observe any people near-by (although don't make it too obvious).
4. Can't go out? Use a room in your house instead.

Second Live Writing Exercise

You'll need a notebook, a pen, a postcard, a camera or smartphone, half a day or a full day to write, and an interesting place to write in.

1. You'll need to plan this in advance. Remember to make up your own rules about what the place should include and how you will approach the exercise.
2. Go to a particular place, such as an interesting building, gardens, a park, an art gallery, or a museum. Write there and then by observing your surroundings. Keep going until you get over ordinary description and then bring in fictional characters to inhabit the space or create interesting images.
3. Ask yourself 'what if?' Imagine an event taking place involving particular fictional characters in the place you have chosen. For example, in my flash fiction story 'The Swim' (written in Kensington Gardens) a character goes for a swim in a duck pond. Alternatively pair everyday / unusual images together.
4. Sit in a particular place with a postcard you

have chosen and write a micro-story on the reverse *as if you were a character* or write a prose poem about the place.
5. Take a series of photographs and write a story or three poems linked to the photographs.

Discussion

What happened when you went out somewhere for half a day / a day to write? How did you feel beforehand? What did you write? Have you turned it into anything?

Want more?

Rather than generally observing, do something specific in the space. Take a friend and sit in front of a sculpture or go on a train journey or a boat trip or walk through a forest listening for sounds or experience a piece of music live, and write during the experience. Compare notes with your friend.

Summary of week seven

When you 'write live', you go to a particular and write there and then about the space you are in. You could also call this technique 'writing in situ'. As well as being inspired by the place, you also observe the minute details. This is an extended writing activity – it might take a few hours or even a whole day. Look after yourself while you do it, and come up with some rules (like 'there must be somewhere to get tea' for instance) before you go.

When you first try Live Writing, go out for forty minutes and see what happens. Sometimes Live Writing is done on a journey or as part of a walk, and involves multiple modes of recording the journey / walk, such as photography or drawing. A few years ago, I wrote a whole series of short stories by visiting places and writing while I was there.

Works Cited

Tondeur, Louise. 'The Swim'. *Unusual Places,* Cultured Llama, 2018. Find out more about how I wrote *Unusual Places* here: https://www.louisetondeur.co.uk/behind-the-scenes/about-unusual-places-book/

Week Eight: Wordplay

What is wordplay and why use it?

Wordplay simply means playing with words. It involves games you play by yourself, with one other person, or in groups. We use wordplay for a variety of reasons. Firstly, wordplay lets us off the hook and allows us to confront our internal censor who says our writing is 'silly'. As creative people, it's important not to get too serious, to allow ourselves to play, to allow ourselves to realise that creativity is playful. Through play, we return to a child-like appreciation of the world. We also use wordplay get words down, which can help with an existing project or with idea generation.

Isn't it all a bit childish?

Sometimes wordplay can be seen as childish and a waste of time. Rob Pope talks about that kind of suspicion of playing in his book *Creativity* (2005). Cynical about playing? Read what he says in the section on play, even if you don't read the whole book, before you reject playing out of hand. It is eye-opening. Often, using wordplay, we come up with unusual words and phrases that are highly productive, even though at first we resisted playing and didn't understand why we were doing it.

Because the playful side of creativity is (unfortunately) often drummed out of us in school, it's through wordplay that we rediscover it. It's easy to try to reach for logic or sense with these writing games but that's not the point, generating words and finding new ways of seeing is more important. Trust the process, at least for a while.

Be a word game magpie

I encourage you to make up your own games and to be like a magpie: to collect writing games you see online, in magazines, or those you experience in workshops. Make a scrapbook. Share your findings with others.

Taking it to extremes

Some writers have taken word games to great extremes. Have a look on the Language is a Virus website for some examples, such as cut up technique and OuLiPo. Or read the beginning of Hazel Smith's *The Writing Experiment* for her take on word association.

Where to start with wordplay

Word association is a good one to start with: pick a random word and write down whatever word comes up for you as a result of thinking it (without dwelling on the first word), and repeat. Play this with a friend if you can.

What next?

1. Now have a go at cut up, and OuLiPo. They'll help break you out of 'making sense' mode.
2. Try writing a list of what you can see. For example, fireplace, table, TV, toys, trunk, water, and then pairing words that don't usually go together.

Make lists

Think about the last journey you went on. Come up with a list of words to describe it. Repeat with a memory of a journey from your childhood. Repeat with an unpleasant journey. Repeat with a journey in another country. Now pair words from different lists. Try to avoid making sense as much as you can.

Make a spark box

Create a box of ideas out of a tissue box or shoe box. Write lines of overheard conversation, proverbs, images, weather reports, colours, unusual things you experience or see. Cut these up and put them in the box. Turn to your spark box when you need inspiration.

More list exercises

1. Make a random list of things. Phone, desk, banana etc. Create sentences for fun from the results.
2. Choose a random job and make a list of verbs

– things workers do at this job. A chef: beat, boil, bake, sauté, fry.
3. Choose another random job and make another list of verbs. Climb, chop, saw, mend, tend, break, repair.
4. Combine random 'job words' to create and describe new jobs.
5. Combine words from all of your lists. Focus on the sound and rhythm of the words.

You'll find more games and prompts like these in one of the other Small Steps Guides, called *How to Write*.

Discussion

1. Read the section on play in Rob Pope's book on *Creativity* (page 119 onwards) and discuss your feelings about childishness and playfulness.
2. Read and discuss 'The Soap Mandible' – written using OuLiPo.

Want more?

- Try out some Flarf poetry.
- Collect / make up your own word games and share them with your friends. Post or link to them them on a blog.
- Use them to run your own writing workshop.
- Challenge the rest of your class to collect and swap word games.

Summary of week eight

Wordplay simply means playing with words. Play might seem childish, especially as we've been taught not to be playful, but trust the process, you might surprise yourself. Some writers, especially those we might call avant-garde, have taken it to extremes. Cut up technique and OuLiPo are examples.

Read what Rob Pope says in *Creativity* about play before you reject wordplay. We use wordplay to confront our internal censor / judge, to allow ourselves to play, to return to a child-like appreciation of the world, to help with idea generation. Start with word association, then try some of the exercises suggested.

Try to move away from 'making sense' and focus on the sound and rhythm of the words and phrases instead. Try making lists of words and making up new phrases by pairing words that don't necessarily fit together. Collect word games and share them with your friends.

Useful websites

http://www.languageisavirus.com/index.php

https://www.poets.org/poetsorg/text/brief-guide-oulipo

https://www.poets.org/poetsorg/text/brief-guide-flarf-poetry

Works Cited

Pope, Rob. *Creativity: Theory, History, Practice*. Routledge, 2005.

Smith, Hazel. *The Writing Experiment: Strategies for Innovative Creative Writing*. Allen & Unwin, 2005.

Week Nine: Mindfulness

Pay attention

Imagine walking down a street. You can picture any town or village you like. Here are two ways of walking down that street:

1. The Automaton: if I walk down the street hunched over, with a heavy bag, not looking where I'm going, making no eye contact with anyone, I'm on autopilot, like a robot;
2. The Observer: or I could notice things around me, and about myself. I could engage all my senses. I could identify myself with my surroundings or otherwise.

A writer is someone who breaks the 'automaton' cycle, someone who becomes aware, who goes through life paying attention. This quality is known as mindfulness. You probably know that because mindfulness has become pretty fashionable recently.

All of the tools in the toolkit encourage us to look at the world with writer's eyes. They encourage us to be aware of the present moment, and to avoid judgement. In other words, they encourage mindfulness.

What is mindfulness?

Mindfulness is about paying attention to the moment you are in, in a non-critical, curious way. Mindfulness has become a popular concept recently, but while treating mindfulness as if it is a cure-all isn't advisable, it is helpful to think of what it means to be a mindful writer. *The Mindful Writer* by Dinty Moore (2012) is a book about Buddhism and writing, which explores this concept.

The practice of mindfulness is useful generally, but we can also turn it into a specific and pragmatic tool, and use it to deepen our writing. Take a look at the blog post by Bodhipaksa on Wildmind.org if you'd like a fuller definition of mindfulness. The link is at the end of the chapter.

A note about spirituality and writing

Some of the bestselling writing practitioners talk about their own spiritual paths when they discuss the creative process, whilst encouraging us to pay attention and to be writer / observers. Examples include:

- Anne Lamont in *Bird by Bird* (1980),
- Julia Cameron in *The Artist's Way* (1995)
- and Natalie Goldberg in her various books on writing.

However, the application of mindfulness to writing

doesn't have to be spiritual, it can be entirely pragmatic and secular.

Mindfulness exercises

1. If you are in a writing workshop, describe your journey to the workshop, including the specific details. If you are working on your own, describe the last journey you took, be it mundane or a great adventure.
2. You may not think this is true right now, but indulge me for a moment. Being a writer is just like any other job. You turn up and do it. So: you're a writer. What's your working day like? What's your routine? If you are in a writing workshop, this could lead to a discussion about writing as a job, and the routines, systems and roles involved.
3. Read the blog post on inspiration by Mason Currey, called 'John Updike, William Faulkner, Chuck Close: They Didn't Wait for Inspiration' and make a note of what you think of it. The link is at the end of the chapter.
4. Mindfulness has become a cultural object in recent years. When a concept like this becomes fashionable, problems and contradictions arise. For example, in her article Karen Heller describes how one can buy mindful tea, burgers, and a diet, amongst other associated cultural phenomenon! If you're in a workshop group, discuss your own examples and experiences.

Have you turned up today?

'The important thing is to turn up at the page and begin.' (Cameron 2010)

Will faultless, aesthetically-pleasing, 'original', income-generating writing stream from your pen or keyboard if only you could think of an idea? No, for at least two reasons:

1. You have to turn up to the page regularly. For example, try freewriting for half an hour a day for a week – or whatever routine you can manage.
2. Writing is about rewriting, and rewriting, and rewriting. Writing is about craft, not the first draft.

Don't try to be original. Observe instead.

Forget about trying to be innovative, new or original. Writing is a process. What to do instead: observe your local environment, the details of it, observe your emotions, your sense impressions in as much specific detail as possible. Make this a regular practice. Spend time writing it down. Make a promise to yourself to notice and observe, to look at the world with a writer's eyes.

Close Observation

Let's go back to the following close observation activities again, but this time focus on mindfulness. You can time the observations if you like. They can last for a short time (1 or 5 mins), or even as much as 45 mins.

1. Choose any object (mundane, interesting, natural, man-made) and watch it for a while.
2. Now write about what the textures of the object suggest.
3. Observe the object for five more minutes.
4. After the observation, write what you experienced.
5. Look back over all you've done. Underline any phrases or images that you particularly like.
6. Afterwards, ask yourself or a classmate: Was it difficult? Is this the way you usually write? What did you like about it?

Repeat the close observation exercise with a different object. This time focus on using a particular sense and putting that sense experience into words.

The next stage is to go outside and observe something. Set a time limit and some ground rules for yourself. Repeat the above steps. Spend time observing whatever you choose *first* before writing.

Whether we are 'professional observers [...] of the world' (Sontag 2011) or observers of the specific details in our local environment, to write is to observe. The word 'observe' has a visual bias, but as far as mindful writing is concerned it means a tendency towards noticing things, experiencing the details, using all of your senses, being curious, being aware.

More Mindfulness activities to try:

- Close observation on the bus, tube, train or tram. Make some notes on the close specific detail.

- Close observation of your own street. Make some notes on the colours of the front doors, the texture of the pavement, or what you notice about the rubbish, the trees, the wheelie bins.
- Notice a particular colour for a set amount of time. Spend your morning noticing different shades of red or green or blue, for instance, and then write about it.
- Pay attention on a walk (to work, through the park, with the dog) and recording some sense impressions afterwards.
- Create a regular practice. Engaging in deliberate 'paying attention' activities or close observation at least once a week.

Discussion

Here are the tools again. All of them involve mindfulness. Discuss how.

- Freewriting: writing without stopping, without editing, without necessarily making sense.
- Creative Visualisation: holding a picture in your head, then describing it. The alternative is using your senses very specifically to describe the person, place or thing.
- Close observation: watching something very closely for a period of time OR noticing the detail in your everyday life.
- Writing Props: these are objects; found objects, tableaux, or objects that tell a story through their provenance.
- Live Writing: writing while in an interesting place, improvising it on the spot.

- Wordplay: returning to (seemingly) childlike playing, to generate ideas. Messing around with words using games.
- Writers' venues: places in the community or online that are dedicated to writing.

Want more?

- Have a look at Dinty Moore's *The Mindful Writer*.
- Read Oliver Burkeman on daily routines, or Madeleine Bunting or Wendy Ann Greenhalgh on mindfulness.
- In order to think about some of the problems associated with the 'fad' of mindfulness, you might like to take a look at Karen Heller's article in the *Washington Post*.
- Cal Newport's *Deep Work* is also a fascinating read.
- I created a free 'Writing and Mindfulness' Course for New Writing South, which you can find here: https://newwritingsouth-s-school.thinkific.com/courses/writing-and-mindfulness

Summary of week nine

A writer is someone who breaks the 'automaton' cycle, someone who becomes aware, who goes through life paying attention. This quality is known as mindfulness. All of the tools in the toolkit encourage it. Although several writing practitioners do talk about the spiritual side of creativity, mindfulness doesn't have to be spiritual. In part, mindfulness is about the habit of 'turning up' (Cameron

2010), and in part about writers being 'observers […] of the world' (Sontag 2011). You've had a go at some mindfulness exercises, and repeated some of the Close Observation exercises with a focus on mindfulness.

Works Cited

Bodhipaksa. 'What is mindfulness?' [Blog post] Available from: http://www.wildmind.org/applied/daily-life/what-is-mindfulness [Accessed September 2017]

Burkeman, Oliver. 'Rise and shine: the daily routines of history's most creative minds'. *Guardian*, Saturday 5 October 2013. Available from: www.theguardian.com/science/2013/oct/05/daily-rituals-creative-minds-mason-currey/print [Accessed October 2013]

Bunting, Madeleine. 'Why we will come to see mindfulness as mandatory'. *Guardian*. Tuesday 6 May 2014. Available from: www.theguardian.com/commentisfree/2014/may/06/mindfulness-hospitals-schools/print [Accessed July 2014]

Cameron, Julia, cited in Fix, Annette. 'The Creative Life: An Interview with Julia Cameron'. Women on Writing, 2010. Available at: www.wow-womenonwriting.com/41-Inspiration-JuliaCameron.html [Accessed August 2015].

Cameron, Julia. *The Artist's Way: The Spiritual Path to Higher Creativity.* Pan, 1995.

Currey, Mason. 'John Updike, William Faulkner, Chuck Close: They Didn't Wait for Inspiration'. [blog post] Available at: www.slate.com/articles/arts/culturebox/features/2013/daily_rituals/john_updike_william_faulkner_chuck_close_they_didn_t_wait_for_inspiration.html [Accessed April 2016].

Goldberg, Natalie. *Writing Down the Bones: Freeing the Writer Within*. Shambhala, 1986.

Greenhalgh, Wendy Ann. 'Mindfulness and writing: We have bodies not just minds'. May 2014. Blog post. Available online at: storyscavenger.blogspot.co.uk/2014/05/mindfulness-and-writing-we-have-bodies.html [Accessed August 2014]

Heller, Karen. (2016) 'When 'mindful' is a mayo, a diet, a mantra, does it actually mean anything?' Washington Post. 8 April 2016.

Lamott, Anne. *Bird by Bird: Instructions on Writing and Life*. Bantam, 1995.

Moore, Dinty. *The Mindful Writer* Wisdom Publications, 2012.

Newport, Cal. *Deep Work: Rules for Success in a Distracted World*. London: Piatkus, 2016.

Sontag, Susan. 'From the 48th Congress of International PEN: Citizens of Language'. *PEN America: A Journal for Writers and Readers.* Issue 14. New York: PEN America. 2011. Pp. 99- 100.

Week Ten: Can Creative Writing Be Taught?

A familiar debate

Can Creative Writing be taught? What do you think, taking into account the activities you've done so far, including the couple of times I suggested that you teach someone else your writing process, or part of it? This is a debate you will most likely come across if you study Creative Writing, or read about how to do it, so let's tackle it head on.

Exercises

1. Based on the activities you've worked through so far, write some notes on your own creative processes. How do you 'think like a writer'? What do you do when you're 'being creative'? (This is a fascinating question, and one that probably has no final answer for any of us.)
2. Now take what you have written and turn it

into a couple of practical writing activities that you could share with and explain to another writer or creative person.
3. If you are working in a group or in a seminar, take the opportunity to teach the practical writing activities you came up with to someone else. If you are working on your own, find a friend to experiment on – perhaps they could teach you a skill in exchange.

Is it possible to teach someone to be creative?

A plethora of writers and researchers have written about creativity and what it means, and what it means to teach it to others. For example, the works of Anna Craft, Rob Pope, Robert Sternberg and Paul Torrance give the lie to the notion that creativity is somehow indefinable and inaccessible. The body of literature investigating creativity and education is so robust that it is almost embarrassing to hear this popular idiom repeated.[1]

For a discussion of how the key arguments apply to Creative Writing, have a look at the opening of Paul Dawson's *Creative Writing and the New Humanities* (2004), chapter 7 of Rob Pope's *Creativity* (2005) and the introduction to Michelene Wandor's *The Author Is Not Dead, Merely Somewhere Else* (2008).

So questions about whether writing specifically can be taught have already been written about in detail by many people but still tend to crop up regularly in British newspapers. A fairly recent example originated with Hanif Kureishi, and was repeated across various media outlets.[2]

Typical of this kind of argument is that referred to by Claire Armitstead writing in the *Guardian* after Martin Amis was made Professor at Manchester (Armitstead

2007), and often the media returns to the debate when a famous writer is appointed in this way. In this repetitive discourse, a critique of what one might call a 'commodification framework', that, by the way, one could apply to the whole of Higher Education, is targeted at the creative arts, and at Creative Writing in particular.

Creative thinking and doing are essential in today's climate

The reiteration of a question like this in the media has an impact on Creative Writing tutors and students, and it also has implications for the way both creative education and teaching are perceived culturally. But, if I may, I would like to propose that the issue has wider ramifications and is therefore even more important. Creative thinking and doing are essential in today's socio-economic and cultural climate. In our current economic situation, and given the serious problems facing society in general, creativity ought to be highly sought after. The implications are too important to ignore.

As I've said, it's been firmly established that creativity can be taught. It's not a mystery. More than ever, we need to learn how to think and act creatively, and Creative Writing programmes have a role in that process. Couple this with what Anders Ericsson (1993) says about expertise – that one can learn the creative arts through 'deliberate practice' – it becomes even more apparent that we need to emphasise the teaching of creative thinking and doing *that we actually already know how to teach*.

As Tim Clare illustrates so memorably in a blog post called 'Can Creative Writing Be Taught? Not If Your Teacher's A Prick', misunderstanding about whether writing can be taught hinges on the words taught or teach, because 'teach' is treated as if it is passive.[3] Plus, the question 'is it possible to teach Creative Writing?' suggests a rather clichéd figure of a writer, a tortured genius and a kind of writing that it is not possible to learn.

Pointing out that there are particular technicalities of writing which can be passed on, or that 'self-expression' is not enough without redrafting, or suggesting that courses provide a framework for students to practise their writing and to read, although honest and pragmatic, is not a full enough answer because, at least on some occasions, the question implies, before it has been answered by anyone who knows about it, that Creative Writing is a commodity being sold to unsuspecting students. Meanwhile so called traditional subjects are not read in a similar way.

Ironically those espousing this point of view give no credence or voice to the student writers themselves, or to the idea that one might learn writing for a variety of reasons. After many years of teaching experience, I can tell you categorically that not everyone studying writing wants to be a published novelist, just as not everyone studying Drama wants to be an actor.

Shifting focus from the 'great' writer as teacher

Another facet of the contradictions that circulate around this question of whether Creative Writing can be taught can be understood from the end of Rachel Cusk's article 'In praise of the creative writing course' (Cusk 2013). There she describes an outburst from a writer upset by the rise of Creative Writing courses. In the article you can read a fear of the democratisation of creative writing. That he particularly wishes to exclude housewives and old women is additionally troubling, but not surprising, given that aspects of the writing scene can also be androcentric. It is not only those with similar anxiety about being classed 'real' writers who reiterate this idiom. Others with a vested interest may want to keep writers special, distant, separate and mysterious.

If we take this into consideration, we no longer have a question about whether writing can be taught, but rather we discover the existence of an antagonistic paradigm that does not want it to be taught, where writing is a secret and only the worthy deserve admittance. But reading Tim Clare's rebuttal of Kureishi soon makes the whole debate about teaching creative writing seem redundant. Clare allows us to look at the argument the other way round. It is simply not the case that it is impossible to teach creativity or writing, but rather, only experienced teachers know how to do it. Clare's article facilitates a shift in focus away from the idea of the 'great writer' as teacher.

Writing for multiple reasons

Unfortunately, a reductive paradigm about learning and teaching writing, as Cusk's troubled writer attests, appears to preclude many of the motivations for writing. There are many reasons to write. Writing for publication is only one of those reasons. Anyone who tells you otherwise is flatly wrong. Writing for wellbeing is one motivation. Look into the work of Lapidus, for example. Creative Writing teaches effective communication. How many times have you watched the news to discover that the root of a serious, often tragic, problem was a lack of good communication?

Communication, far from being a 'soft' skill, is key to solving many local and global problems. It isn't even really a 'skill', but rather a life's work, something one embodies. (Take a look at Oren Jay Sofer's book *Say What You Mean*, if you're interested in exploring this idea further.) I am not trying to claim that the teaching of Creative Writing is a solution to all difficult and complex problems, of course, but it does have at least a part to play.

And why not write for the sake of it, like you might dance or sing? I must say that, when I first started, I never thought of coming up with a reason to write: I simply wanted to do it. I couldn't help myself.

Let's look at how instead

Let's move away from circular debates about whether writing can be learnt and taught and instead look *how* creative writing is learnt and taught. I've got space for two 'hows' here: rhizomatic learning and contingency.

Rhizomatic learning

If you've read this far, then you probably agree that the following is a reductive cultural idiom; that it is problematic to treat teaching as if it involves the receipt of a skill by a learner, via some kind of dissemination, in what, in some contexts, is an economic exchange.[4] The learner pays, the teacher imparts knowledge. This is a highly limited and limiting view of learning and teaching anyway, but especially in a creative context.

Creative learning and teaching involves a dialogue between student and teacher through a variety of planned interactions, including conversations between learner and teacher and opportunities for the student to shape the learning. For instance, David Cormier writes about rhizomatic education where learning is 'negotiated' and continually overlaps with other forms of knowing (Cormier 2008):

'A botanical metaphor, first posited by Deleuze and Guattari in *A Thousand Plateaus* (1987), may offer a more flexible conception of knowledge for the information age: the rhizome. A rhizomatic plant has no center and no defined boundary; rather, it is made up of a number of semi-independent nodes, each of which is capable of growing and spreading on its own […] In the rhizomatic view, knowledge can only be negotiated.'

Where it might seem sensible and appropriate to follow a systematic delivery of teaching involving policy, planning, dissemination, evaluation and feedback, creative learning and teaching involves the unexpected, learning in the moment, learning from the interaction between the people present in the room, but also from the circumstance itself.

Contingency in a creative learning environment

Contingency in a creative learning environment is similar to, although not exactly the same as, the way in which one might understand a performance or a piece of art in the moment, an encounter that can only be partially described and reflected upon, but not repeated, once the moment has past. Contingency does not necessarily involve a lack of planning, although one way to try it is for a tutor to include one or two unplanned sessions in a term, but rather, a different attitude to the process. One allows for disjuncture, change and new meanings to emerge.

To support this idea, let's own the fact that session outlines involving creative practice look rather mundane on the page. They only come to life when writer-teacher and writer-student experience the activities together; in other words, contingency gives life to the learning process.

Discussion

- How would you teach Creative Writing if you were in charge of a class for a term / semester?
- What does contingency mean to you?
- What is a rhizome and how could it be used to teach creative thinking or communication skills?

Want more?

Take a look at Tim Clare's blog post on whether it's possible to teach creative writing (2014), and at what Anders Ericsson says about 'deliberate practice' (1993).

Summary of week ten

The question 'Can you teach Creative Writing?' or a variation of it, comes up again and again in the popular press, and effects how we think about writing. Although this usually isn't acknowledged, a whole host of people have written about teaching creativity. Creative thinking and doing – and learning how to do it – are really important, given the way the world is right now.

David Cormier writes about rhizomatic education where learning is 'negotiated' and continually overlaps with other forms of knowing (Cormier 2008), which is a good way of looking at learning creativity. Also important, contingency is an encounter that can only be partially described and reflected upon, but not repeated, once the moment has past.

Works Cited

Armitstead, Claire. 'Can Creative Writing Be Taught?' *Guardian*, Saturday 17 February 2007. Available at: <http://www.theguardian.com/lifeandstyle/2007/feb/17/weekend.clairearmitstead/print> [Accessed February 2014].

Buckingham, Will. 'Hanif Kureishi is wrong about students: There are talents in everyone, and it is the teacher's role to develop them'. *Times Higher*. 13 March, 2014. Available at: www.timeshighereducation.com/comment/opinion/hanif-kureishi-is-wrong-about-students/2011965.article [Accessed April 2016].

Clare, Tim. 'Can Creative Writing Be Taught? Not If Your Teacher's A Prick'. 5 March 2014. [blog post] Available at: www.timclarepoet.co.uk/?p=2236 [Accessed April 2016].

Clark, Nick and Alice Jones. 'The Independent Bath Literature Festival: Creative writing courses are a waste of time, says Hanif Kureishi (who teaches one)'. *Independent*. 3 March 2014. Available at: www.independent.co.uk/arts-entertainment/books/news/the-independent-bath-literature-festival-creative-writing-courses-are-a-waste-of-time-says-hanif-9166697.html [Accessed April 2016].

Cormier, David. 'Rhizomatic Education: Community as Curriculum', in *Innovate* 4:5, 2008. Available at: davecormier.com/edblog/2008/06/03/rhizomatic-education-community-as-curriculum [Accessed November 2013].

Craft, Anna and Bob Jeffrey. 'Teaching Creatively and Teaching for Creativity: Distinctions and Relationships.' *Educational Studies*. Vol. 30.1, 2004, pp. 77-87.

Cusk, Rachel. 'In Praise of the Creative Writing Course'. *Guardian*. 18 January 2013. Available at: www.

theguardian.com/books/2013/jan/18/in-praise-creative-writing-course [Accessed January 2013].

Dawson. Paul. *Creative Writing and the New Humanities*. London: Routledge, 2004.

Dixon, Hayley. 'Creative writing courses are a waste of time'. *Telegraph*. 4 March 2014. Available at: www.telegraph.co.uk/culture/books/10674887/Creative-writing-courses-are-a-waste-of-time-says-Hanif-Kureishi.html [Accessed April 2016].

Flood, Alison. Creative writing professor Hanif Kureishi says such courses are 'a waste of time'. *Guardian*. 4 March 2014. Available at: www.theguardian.com/books/2014/mar/04/creative-writing-courses-waste-of-time-hanif-kureishi [Accessed April 2016].

Kureishi, Hanif. 'What they don't teach you at Creative Writing school'. *Telegraph*. 25 January 2014. Available at: www.telegraph.co.uk/culture/books/10594606/Hanif-Kureishi-What-they-dont-teach-you-at-creative-writing-school.html [Accessed April 2016].

Kim, Kyung Hee. 'Can We Trust Creativity Tests? A Review of the Torrance Tests of Creative Thinking'. *Creativity Research Journal*. Vol. 18.1, 2006, pp. 3-14.

Pope, Rob. *Creativity: Theory, History, Practice*, London: Routledge, 2005.

Sofer, Oren Jay. *Say What You Mean*. Boulder, Colorado: Shambhala, 2018.

Sternberg, Robert. 'The Nature of Creativity'. *Creativity Research Journal*. Vol. 18, No. 1, 2006, pp. 87–98.

Wandor, Michelene. *The Author Is Not Dead, Merely Somewhere Else: Creative Writing after Theory: Creative Writing Reconceived*. Basingstoke: Palgrave, 2008.

[unknown] 'Kureishi slams creative writing courses'. *The Bookseller*. 4th March 2014. [web article] Available

online at: www.thebookseller.com/news/kureishi-slams-creative-writing-courses [Accessed April 2016.]

[unknown] 'Teaching creative writing a 'waste of time''. BBC World Update. 7th March 2014. [Radio broadcast] www.bbc.co.uk/programmes/p01tg8q2

Notes

[1] See, for instance, Craft and Jeffrey 2004, Kim 2006, Pope 2005 and Sternberg 2006.

[2] See, for instance, Alice Jones and Nick Clark in the *Independent*, and Hayley Dixon in the *Telegraph*, and Alison Flood in the *Guardian* plus Will Buckingham's response in the *Times Higher*, or the article from Kureishi himself in the *Telegraph*.

[3] See Clare 2014, and Clark and Jones 2014.

[4] I am reminded here of the images of the robot teacher at Jiujiang University that circulated on social media a few years ago.

PART II

Developing your practice

Week One - Three: Creative Journeys

Going on a journey

We've talked about journeys before during this book and in this chapter, I start with some thoughts about why 'the journey' is used as a metaphor for the writing process, and I suggest that you go on an actual journey and record the process. During week one, do your research – prepare to go on your journey and decide what you will write. During week two, go on your journey and record what happens. Write up and edit the results. If you can, during week three, share what happened and what you wrote as a result with your group or with a friend. If you can't go on an actual journey, go on one in your imagination or research a journey online.

Writing as a journey

You might have heard people say it's the journey that's important, not the destination. By doing so, they are foregrounding *process*. Many creative people argue that it's the creative process, not the end result, that's the most important aspect for them. What about you?

A journey has definite stages to it: you get ready, you set off, you encounter difficulties and respond to them along the way, you reach your destination. Each of these stages is useful when thinking about the writing process. 'Journey' as a metaphor has become a cultural idiom: a recognisable way of talking about the world. Sometimes cultural idioms are so easily repeated that we forget they are there at all. The journey metaphor is one of these very commonly used ideas.

The journey metaphor is often applied to the writer's life. For instance: I'm a beginning writer, I start to experiment, to get more experienced, I publish some work, I encounter obstacles along the way, I become an experienced writer, I keep practising.

In fact, it is almost impossible to describe the creative process without recourse to journey metaphors: sometimes we are flâneurs, wanderers, or pilgrims, and writing practitioners have described journeys across changing landscapes to illustrate writing processes. Julia Cameron does so in *The Sound of Paper* (Cameron 2004. p. 24) for example.

The journey of a writing project

The journey metaphor is also used for longer writing projects. It's a way of understanding the process of writing a screenplay or a nonfiction book or a poetry collection or a novel – I go on a journey and I don't necessarily know where I'm going to end up. The 'destination' is the finished project. The 'journey' is what I do to get there.

You can also use a journey to structure your story.

Joseph Campbell writes about 'The Hero's Journey' (Campbell 1972). For the novelist or screenwriter this can mean your main character going on a 'quest' to solve a problem that's upset the status quo. This can also mean that you write about your character going on an actual journey; many novelists and screenwriters have used this as a structure.

Poets often consider the 'journey' of their pamphlet or collection, and you may have heard writers talk about taking their reader 'on a journey', or agents and editors talk about the publishing 'journey. from idea to bookshelf. Suffice to say, we hear this metaphor a lot!

Because of all these things, journeys help us to understand the writing process. In fact, writing about - or during - journeys can be a really useful exercise. It makes us better observers of life, and better at making the mundane and ordinary 'new' for our readers, remembering it is careful observation plus practice, and not inspiration, that ultimately makes us better writers.

Why your life is not a journey

A journey is, for the Creative Practitioner, a form of mindfulness, a route towards greater awareness and a sense of curiosity in the everyday. However, please listen to 'Why Your Life is Not a Journey' by Alan Watts – this counters the popular idiom that life is a journey, and is also about increasing awareness of the present moment. You can find it on YouTube.

Writing exercise: go on a journey

You're going on a writing journey. This could be a walk, or a train journey, or a bus ride. The key thing is that you can observe as you go, and stop to record your impressions. This is often best done with a friend or in a group.

Prepare for your journey

1. Make some notes preparing for the practical aspects of your journey. Plan your route and have a look at a map of the whole area, for example. Do you have a destination (such as a particular gallery, museum, beach, or café)? Tell someone where you are going and / or take someone with you.
2. Plan how you will record your journey. Will you sketch, for instance, write down sense impressions, or take photographs? Consider what you might write afterwards, and what form it could take. Examples: a flash fiction piece, a series of poems responding to photographs, a page of a screenplay, a magazine article or a blog post.
3. Is there anything you'll need? For example, you could buy some postcards along the way or you could use your phone to take photographs, or take a blanket to sit on.

Record your journey

Record your journey in one or more of the following ways:

- Photographs,
- Lists of words,
- Sense impressions,
- Buying and writing postcards,

- Interviews with local people,
- Sketches,
- Drawing maps,
- Brief notes about the route or the area,
- Writing first drafts of poems or flash fiction,
- Keeping a record of overheard conversations,
- Filming documentary footage.

However you do it, document where you go, so that you can retell the story of your journey later. While you are on your journey, use Close Observation. Observe using all of the senses. Be aware of your surroundings and notice what most people don't see. Find the specific details.

After your journey

Collate the material you have gathered during the journey. You could create a scrapbook, for instance. If you are on a long train journey and have space, you could do some of this work on the train, otherwise wait until you have space to work.

Write a piece responding to an aspect of the journey. This could be in any form. For example, write the beginning of a documentary or a graphic novel, a poem or poems or flash fiction, perhaps accompanied by photographs, a short feature article or a column for a newspaper or magazine, or a short story.

Discussion

Discuss your preparations for the walk, and – once you've written up the results – get together afterwards and run a writing workshop, giving each other feedback.

Want more?

Repeat this activity and collect several writing journeys (several walks, or several train rides, for example). Read more about the role of the flâneur. (I've suggested an article from the *Paris Review* at the end of this chapter to get you started.) Or take a look at Julia Cameron's *The Sound of Paper* and describe her journey.

Summary: weeks one - three

A journey has definite stages to it: you get ready, you set off, you encounter difficulties and respond to them along the way, and this journey metaphor is often applied to the process of writing, narrative structure, the reader's journey and to the writer's life. Prepare for a writing journey, share your plans then go on the journey. Record your journey in one of the ways suggested. After your journey, collate the material you have gathered, write a piece responding to your journey and workshop the results. Alan Watts' 'Why Your Life is Not a Journey' provides some interesting points for discussion.

Works Cited

Cameron, Julia. *The Sound of Paper: Inspiration and Practical Guidance for Starting the Creative Process*. Penguin, 2006.

Campbell, Joseph. *The Hero With a Thousand Faces*. Princeton Bollingen, 1972.

Lindberg, David and Alan Watts. 'Why Your Life Is Not A Journey,' 2016. Available from: www.youtube.com/watch?v=qHnIJeE3LAI [Accessed September 2017]

Stephen, Bijan. 'In Praise of the Flâneur.' *Paris Review*,

October 17, 2013. https://www.theparisreview.org/blog/2013/10/17/in-praise-of-the-flaneur/ [Accessed May 2022]

Week Four: Processes

Why process?

Writing is a process. There's a popular myth in circulation that suggests writers get a sudden surge of inspiration and fire off a few poems or a novel, publish, and collect their reward (or get rejected because no-one understand their true genius). But the process of writing is more complicated than that.

In the last chapter we look at one particular kind of process, the process of a journey. The journey is often used as a metaphor for the writing process and journeys themselves can be productive, because they suggest ideas.

The best way to understand what is meant by the writing process is to compare it to a finished artefact. In other words, a process is different from a finished product. A published book in the reader's hand might be the finished product (although you could argue that the reader has to engage with it first) but the *process* of writing that book was probably full of complications, successes and challenges.

Thinking about process and what it means is particularly useful if you're called on to write a reflective essay as part of your Creative Writing course. It's also useful, in a less academic way, to develop an awareness of your process so you know what works for you and can use it again next time!

If writing is a process, then what are the stages?

If writing is a process, and sometimes a very messy, contradictory one, then it is helpful to know what the stages are. Several years ago I wrote an essay where I attempted to draw the stages in the writing process in three diagrams. I did an 'official' version, a non-causal or semi-cyclical version, and a messy version. You don't need to read the whole essay to get the gist. I'll give you the reference at the end of this chapter. Feel free to use the diagrams if they help.

In the most simple version of the diagram, I call the stages in the process of writing 'idea generation, incubation, planning, research, drafting, redrafting, proofing, submission, critique, redrafting, publication, reflection' (Tondeur 2017).

There is another important stage that I left out and it is what Julia Cameron calls 'artists' dates'. She writes about this tool in various places including *The Artist's Way* (1995) and you can also find out more on her website. Essentially, this part of the process is about being in the world as a writer, and feeding the artist in you with interesting things. Julia Cameron explains Artists Dates on her website here.

When I first showed my diagrams of the writing process to my undergraduate students they took the first one seriously, it was what they were used to hearing, and they started to make notes. When I showed them the third one they laughed, though, because it's a more honest reflection of what actually happens and they all knew it, but we rarely talk about it. Diagram number three, I hope you'll agree, with context, interruptions, and life getting in the way, is more authentic, and if we pretend it isn't then we will continually disappoint ourselves. One of the other Small Steps Guides is about finding time to write, and understanding this idea of context is the key to that too.

Create two lists

1. List different processes. E.g., learning something, putting flat-pack furniture together, planning a wedding, climbing a tree, travelling the world.
2. Now list different *written* processes. For example, a cake recipe, a TV installation instruction manual, instructions on how to play Ludo.
3. Take one of the above. Can you list the different stages in the process? For example, a cake recipe: ingredients, equipment, oven temperature, mixing, baking, decoration.

Creative a third list

This time, name different kinds of *creative* processes. For example, architecture, making a sculpture, writing a poem, designing a mural.

Take one of the above. Can you list the different stages in the process? For example, what are stages are involved in writing a poem? Here are some:

- stimulus or starting point (not necessarily an 'idea'),
- thinking time,
- getting a few words down,
- drafting,
- research,
- redrafting (several times),
- finishing,
- submitting,
- publication,
- marketing.

Do you always get through all of these? Do they necessarily go in this order? Can up think of others?

Discussion

1. Have a look at the three diagrams I drew of the writing process.
2. Discuss what your writing process is like and have a go at drawing it.

Want more?

Spend time finding out about 'Artist Dates', as well as Julia Cameron's other tools, using her website.

Summary: week four

A published book in the reader's hand can be considered a finished product, but writing that book was a *process*. Elsewhere I call the stages in the process of writing 'idea generation, incubation, planning, research, drafting, redrafting, proofing, submission, critique, redrafting, publication, reflection' (Tondeur 2017). However, I've missed out one important aspect – what Julia Cameron calls 'Artist Dates' (1995), and the process, in reality, gets much more messy and complicated. Looking at different processes unrelated to writing, like recipes or climbing a tree, can help you to understand how they work.

Works Cited

Cameron, Julia. *The Artist's Way: The Spiritual Path to Higher Creativity.* Pan, 1995. http://juliacameronlive.com/basic-tools/artists-dates/ [Accessed September 2017.]

Tondeur, Louise. 'Risk, constraint, play: A new paradigm for examining practice-research in the academy.' *TEXT: Journal of Writing and Writing Courses.* Available at: http://www.textjournal.com.au/april17/tondeur.htm [Accessed September 2017.] (Scroll down to see the three diagrams.)

Week Five: Storyboarding

What is storyboarding?

Storyboards are used in TV, film and animation, to suggest how each shot will be framed. However, in its simplest form, storyboarding involves creating frames (boxes) that will illustrate the progress of your writing project, using drawings or words, like a comic strip. This form of storyboarding employs the writer's firm friend 'What If?' (repeatedly), and also asks What? Where? Who? How? Why? Storyboarding makes use of cause and effect, which is why it's good for structure and sequencing, two things student writers often find hard.

A visual representation

A storyboard is a visual representation of the writing process. Visual representations can help us to see a writing project as a whole. Sticky notes on your wall, or index cards, can create a visual representation too, or you can draw your writing project on a large sheet of paper, or create a mind map. (*Use Your Head* by Tony Buzan is an accessible guide if you'd like to learn to mind map.)

Storyboarding exercise

Use a combination of words and pictures for this creative exercise. I suggest you have a go at drawing, even if only stick figures. (If drawing is your thing, you can get really creative here.) Add key words and phrases. You can of course use this technique to help you to visualise a story you are already working on, although in the example below I encourage you to plan a new piece as you go along, so you can see how it works.

You're going to start to plan a piece of crime fiction. The genre doesn't really matter but for the sake of this writing activity, I chose crime because it tends to have a very clear beginning, middle and end. First of all, decide what *form* the final version will take. Will it be a comic book, flash fiction, novel, screenplay or short story? You don't have to commit to finishing it – this is just meant as a fun game, and so you know how to plan it. Make some notes as follows:

1. A crime takes place. What is it? Jot it down.
2. Decide where the crime takes place.
3. Come up with three or four characters who will inhabit the world – this is your 'who?' Give them jobs.
4. Who are the suspects? Decide who did it.
5. Come up with a detective character – give them a part-time day job as well.
6. How is the crime committed and *why*?
7. What happens next? What complicates the story?

8. What obstacles does the main character face?
9. What's the resolution? Do they get caught?
10. How does the whole thing end?

By the way, if you're interested in writing crime fiction for children, you might like to look into the prize-winning Adventures on Trains series by M.G. Leonard and Sam Sedgman.

Create your storyboard

Now we're going to storyboard your crime story based on your notes. Start with 6 – 8 frames (or boxes) – you can set these up in a Word Document or draw them yourself. Put more in as you need them.[1]

1. On your storyboard create the 'world' (location, specifics) in the first frame.
2. The next frame contains the crime itself, taking place in the moment (i.e. not reported later).
3. Now use your middle frames to show complications. Use the power of *What If?*
4. The final frame is the resolution – what happens in the end? Fill in that frame now. Think specifics.

Sometimes it's easier to do the final frame at step 3 and to fill in the middle as the final step, because that way you know what you're working towards.

Discussion

Come up with a list of the various ways you can represent your writing visually. The key thing is to illustrate the whole picture, that is, the whole novel or play or screenplay, for instance. Take a look at this newspaper article showing Will Self's writer's room[2] (or how it was in 2007 anyway) for an example of the use of (a kind of) visual representation. or learn more about crime writer Victoria Dowd's use of a 'Murder Board'.[3]

Want more?

Have a look at some storyboards created for TV shows. For example, you can view storyboards from Dr Who on the BBC website.[4] Try coming up with a visual representation of your work in progress, or create a storyboard illustrating a writer's career as if it were a journey.

Summary of week five

In its simplest form, storyboarding involves creating frames that will illustrate the progress of your writing project, using drawings or words. Your storyboard is a visual representation of the writing process. Visual representations can help us to see a writing project as a whole. Use a combination of words and pictures to make up the outline for a piece of crime fiction. Follow the guidelines to make notes on your story first, and then storyboard it. Even if you end up with stick figures, include some drawing.

Works Cited

Buzan, Tony. *Use Your Head: How to Unleash the Power of Your Mind*. London: BBC Active, 2010.

Notes

[1] Tutors can download free storyboarding templates from this website: https://www.twinkl.co.uk/resource/t-l-2162-storyboard-templates

[2] The link to the picture is here: https://www.theguardian.com/books/2007/apr/06/writers.rooms.will.self

[3] Victoria Dowd's discusses her use of a 'Murder Board' in this interview: https://www.writing.ie/interviews/the-golden-road-to-publication-the-smart-womans-guide-to-murder-by-victoria-dowd/

[4] See the Doctor Who storyboard here: http://www.bbc.co.uk/programmes/p01nhdbj/p01nhcvy

Week Six: Rewriting the Myths of Success and Failure

Stories about creative success and failure

Here are some stories we tell about success: We're either successful or we're not. We're either talented or we're not. To be successful you need luck. Success is a stable, fixed state. You succeed and stay successful. Failure is the opposite of success.

Here are some stories we tell about failure: Failure is a bad thing. Failure must be avoided at all costs. Talented people never fail at anything. Failure is a personal trait, as in 'I am a failure.' Once you've failed it's hard to succeed. Failure is the opposite of success.

None of the above stories of success and failure are actually true. If you look behind the hype, what all successful people have in common is that they (and often their parents and grandparents) failed multiple times.

Telling a baby to give up trying to walk and talk

Would you tell a baby that he or she is a failure if s/he didn't learn to walk first time? Unlikely. Look at it this way: When babies try to walk, do they give up after the first time they fall over? No, they get up over and over until they succeed. Exactly the same thing happens when those babies and try out words for the first time.

How bizarre it would be if the first time a child tried to walk or speak we said 'That's it, you've failed at walking and talking now. You may as well give up.' Yet we sometimes berate ourselves for 'failing' at the thing we really want to do, be it getting our work published, or finding a dream job, or whatever we see as success.

The usefulness of trial and error

We've forgotten about the usefulness of trial and error. It's one of the most beneficial learning tools around, and you already know how. It's been working for you since you learnt to walk and talk. Humans evolved to learn through failure. A mistake is useful because it allows us to amend a process and try again with a slightly different approach, and repeat. We try something out, adapt and improve, then we try again, and adapt again.

Those terrible first drafts

The same thing applies to the writing process. We can't expect to get our writing 'perfect' in a first draft. Aim to get something down even if it is imperfect. In fact, it is better to aim for imperfection in your first draft if the alternative means staring at your computer screen writing nothing at all. (You might find that your 'terrible' first draft isn't as terrible as you think it is.) Write and edit one short story and the next one will be better as a result. The key to success is practice and not innate talent. And if you haven't yet read Anne Lamott essay called 'Shitty First Drafts' in *Bird by Bird*, look it up; it might surprise you.

Carol Dweck and 'mindsets'

According to Carol Dweck (2012), people with a 'growth mindset' have a different reaction to failure to those with a 'fixed mindset'. 'Growth mindset' people see challenges as an opportunity to learn and grow.

Because they approach setbacks this way, 'growth mindset' people might, for instance, set up several processes knowing some will fail but some will succeed, in the same way that a gardener might nurture several seedlings knowing only some will fully mature.

Say two writers submitted a short story to a magazine and both are rejected. The writer with the 'fixed' mindset might well blame themselves, and put the story away for good, without even reading the note from the editor. The writer with a 'growth mindset' will let themselves feel upset, wait a while, revise the story, do some research on short story outlets, and submit the work somewhere else.

A new formula for success

These ideas about failure and success have struck a chord with many writers, this one included, because the quotation from Samuel Beckett's *Worstward Ho!* 'fail again, fail better' has become something of a mantra. Andrew Cowan talks about it in the introduction to *The Art of Writing Fiction*, for instance.

To reverse the 'success myths' outlined at the start, we

can instead think of a formula for success going something like this: fail / try again / get a bit better / fail / try again / get a bit better / fail / try again / get a bit better / success / more success. It's not going to go in a straight line like this, of course.

Effort you put in ages ago might lead to a result in the future. A story that's been hidden in a drawer might spark an idea for a screenplay. 10 CVs sent out on spec might yield two results in a week or in a year's time. Writing ideas that have been brewing in the backs of our minds might come to fruition only when the environment is right. This new formula for success is actually a tried and tested formula for success, so easy babies do it every day, in every country around the world.

Revision exercise

Look out some writing you've done in the past (maybe it's been rejected, or you gave up on it) and decide if there are any nuggets in there you can 'mine' for a future piece of work. What did / didn't work about this piece of writing?

Discussion

Come up with some examples of processes that work better with trial and error. How can you apply a 'growth mindset' to your writing life?

Want more?

Read Carol Dweck's book *Mindset* and the first chapter of Andrew Cowan's *The Art of Writing Fiction*. Or take a look at *The Successful Author Mindset* by Joanna Penn.

Summary of week six

We tell ourselves various stories about success and failure, but they're actually not true. What all successful people have in common is that they failed multiple times. Would you tell a baby that he or she is a failure if s/he didn't learn to walk first time? Unlikely! A mistake is useful because it allows us to amend a process and try again with a slightly different approach. We try something out, adapt and improve, then we try again, and adapt again.

According to Carol S. Dweck, people with a 'growth mindset' see challenges as an opportunity to learn and grow. Instead of the old repetitive stories about creative success and failure, let's create a new formula for success; actually it's not new at all, it's as old as humanity.

Works Cited

Becket, Samuel, *Worstward Ho!*, Grove Press, 1984.

Cowan, Andrew. *The Art of Writing Fiction*. Routledge, 2011.

Dweck, Carol. *Mindset: How You Can Fulfil Your Potential*. New York: Robinson, 2012.

Lamott, Anne. *Bird by Bird: Instructions on Writing and Life*. Bantam, 1995.

Penn, Joanna. *The Successful Author Mindset*. Curl Up Press, 2016.

Week Seven to Ten: The Journey from Idea to Bookshelf

What is this chapter about?

Here's one final project to have a go at: set up a small press and launch a book into the world, taking your book from idea to bookshelf – one of the journeys we touched on earlier.

If you don't want to do this for real then *imagine* you were going to launch a book, and take a look at the steps you would need to take.

I suggest that you spend four weeks preparing for this project. To give you an idea of time frame for the rest of the work, allow yourself three months from the point where you have all the writing finished and edited. So if the writing is done and edited in April, you might plan to launch in July. Work this out from the get go as it will give you a timetable. And remember that launching a book requires project management skills and editing skills in equal measure.

What kind of book will you produce?

You can choose of course, but for the purpose of this example, let's say that the book is either:

- An anthology of local writers, or those in your writing / reading group
- An anthology of writing from around the world, using a website to call for submissions
- An anthology of writing from others in your class

The Set Up

First of all, what would you need to do to set up your small press?

- Who is involved?
- What will you call your press?
- What roles will you need to assign?
- Do you have a budget? How much?
- Who is going to help?
- What needs to be designed?
- What needs to be purchased? (Software like Vellum, for instance, or a domain name.)
- What advice do you need? (Legal advice, small business set up advice, help creating your final product, help from someone who's done it before?)
- What services do you need to search for? That is, what can't you do easily yourself? (A printer, for instance)
- What key decisions do you need to take? (Choosing content and format: ebook or print

copy or both, for example, or deciding who will create the website and which platform to use.)
- Decide on your various deadlines and the launch date for the book.

The Task List

Secondly, what tasks do you need to perform in order to create and launch the book? You can divide this into separate areas of attention, such as the following. Many of these will be going on in tandem.

- The call for submissions, if relevant
- The website
- The process of writing
- The selection process
- Communication with writers / your team
- Editing the content
- ISBNs and registration of press
- Do you need a barcode?
- Selecting and working with contributors
- Cover layout and design, including back matter and spine
- Internal book layout and design
- Web design and blogging
- Marketing (including organising the launch)
- Organising readings and events around the book
- Converting your ebook
- Handing over the book to your POD (print on demand) company. Or uploading to publishing services such as Lulu, KDP or Draft2Digital.
- Handling stock and selling
- Hiring staff / finding volunteers

- Seeking advice

Specific steps

Work backwards from your launch date, what specific steps will you need to take to launch your book? Give yourself some planning time and schedule the rest of your steps.

Resources

- Alliance of Independent Authors (Alli): www.allianceindependentauthors.org Alli produce several guides including the most recent edition of 'How to Choose a Self-Publishing Service'.
- Book Funnel: authors.bookfunnel.com/faq
- Calibre (ebook service): https://calibre-ebook.com/
- Canva: www.canva.com
- The Creative Penn: www.thecreativepenn.com
- Draft2Digital: www.draft2digital.com
- Gimp (image manipulation software): https://www.gimp.org/
- Ingram Spark: www.ingramspark.com/how-it-works
- Jane Friedman: www.janefriedman.com
- The Kindlepreneur: https://kindlepreneur.com
- Lulu: https://www.lulu.com
- Mslexia, and their guide to Indie Presses:https://mslexia.co.uk/writing-guides/independent-press-guide/
- 100 Covers (who did the cover for this book) https://100covers.com/

- Small Publishers Fair (London, UK): smallpublishersfair.co.uk
- Toast Guide to Starting a Small Press (from 2014): http://the-toast.net/2014/03/12/guide-to-starting-a-small-press
- Vellum (software I used to create this book): https://vellum.pub/

Discussion

- What are some of the pitfalls of working in a team and how could you seek to address them from the start of the process?
- If you were to write a guide to the process of publishing an anthology, what would the chapters be called?
- Discuss access requirements and making your launch event accessible to all.

Want more?

Get hold of Jane Friedman's *Publishing 101* and Joanna Penn's *Successful Self-Publishing* for some frank advice about publishing a book. There are more links to books and websites in the resources chapter in the Small Steps Guide called *How to Write a Novel and Get It Published*.

Summary: weeks seven to ten

You are going to set up a small press and launch a book into the world (or imagine you are going to launch a book and discuss the process in class). First of all, what would you need to do to set up your small press? What will you call it, and what roles will you need to assign, for example? Next decide which tasks you will need to perform in order to create and launch the book, taking into account the resources listed in this chapter.

Works Cited

Friedman, Jane. *Publishing 101: A First-Time Author's Guide*. MBA for Writers, 2014.

Glammatteo, Jim and Orna Ross. *How to Choose a Self-Publishing Service*. Alli, 2017.

Penn, Joanna. *Successful Self-Publishing*. Curl Up Press, 2015.

Tondeur, Louise. *How to Write a Novel and Get It Published*. Small Steps, 2017. https://www.louisetondeur.co.uk/how-to-write-a-novel-and-get-it-published/

How to Organise a Literary Event

Literary events: the basics

Assuming you now have a book to launch, in this chapter we'll discuss how to organise a literary event and why it's easier than you think if you break it down into small steps. Here are the basics:

- First of all: go to literary events. This sounds obvious but this is how you gain the tacit knowledge you need. This applies to online events too. Go most of all because you enjoy it and want to support the writers involved. Go to check out the venue and the set up. Go because it's a good way to meet people.
- Go to literary events that are outside your comfort zone: in a new venue, a different kind of writing, a different approach to the topic. How do they do it differently?
- Use your local library, independent bookshops, community centres, writing centres and / or

online writing spaces. Tap into the on or offline writing community. These are good sources of information; getting to know people will help.
- Remember that literary events aren't only about big festivals and household names. Check out small presses and local festivals. Build your network. Use social media.
- Volunteer to help promote an event you like or help m.c. (introduce the speakers) after you've been going for a while.
- Organise an informal reading event for you and your friends.
- Join a writing group and put on an event at your local library or on Zoom.

Your first team meeting

Organise a team meeting and get to know each other. Here are some initial tasks, which could form an agenda for your first meeting:

- Use the resources already out there. Find your nearest writers' centre. In the UK, for instance, there are several regional writing organisations. Check out their websites for resources. The National Poetry Library website is great for resources too. Do some research and compile a list of writing organisations in your part of the world.
- Know what you want to achieve. Organising an event doesn't have to cost a lot of money. At the other extreme, literary programming can be a business venture, involving investment and

everything else that goes along with setting up a business.
- Write down clearly what you want to achieve and what steps you think you need to get there. Include research or planning. What roles will you need to fill? Keeping it all in your head isn't an option!

Research pointers

Develop your own leads depending on the part of the world you're in. I've given you a handful of links below. There are many more, including international ones, many of which I've included in the resources section of the Small Steps Guide called *How to Write a Novel and Get It Published*, but your initial research should send you on a bit of a detective trail, and you'll discover more leads as you go.

You can find out about literary festivals here: https://www.welovebookfestivals.com/festival-calendar

If you're in the North of England, have a look at New Writing North: http://newwritingnorth.com/

Writing East Midlands is here: https://writingeastmidlands.co.uk/

Writing West Midlands is here: https://writingwestmidlands.org/

If you're in London, try Spread the Word: https://www.spreadtheword.org.uk/

In the South East of England, check out New Writing South: https://www.newwritingsouth.com/

For the South West, take a look at Literature Works: https://literatureworks.org.uk/

The National Poetry Library is here: http://www.poetrylibrary.org.uk/

The Scottish Poetry Library is here: http://www.

scottishpoetrylibrary.org.uk/

The Scottish Writers' Centre is here: https://scottishwriterscentre.co.uk/

The National Writing Centre of Wales is here: https://www.tynewydd.wales/

The National Writers' Centre for England is here: https://nationalcentreforwriting.org.uk/

A few years ago Creative Future in Brighton published a *Pathway Guide for Writers* with lots of links to literary organisations in the UK. You can and you can download it from this page on their website for a small fee: https://www.creativefuture.org.uk/resource/pathway-guide-for-writers/

If you're in North America, take a look at the AWP website: https://www.awpwriter.org/ or check out the resources on the Write Life website, such as: https://thewritelife.com/best-websites-for-writers-2021/

Take action

So you're ready to go? What next?

- Once you've done your research, organise another meet up with your team. Assign roles, set deadlines, set goals. Be as specific as possible.
- Meet regularly and check up on those goals. Even if you're working by yourself, still do this! Meet with yourself regularly.

Event subheadings

All events have general aspects in common. For instance:

- Audience
- Budgeting
- Catering and refreshment
- Customs and traditions (i.e. the structure of the event, things that tend to happen at the literary events you enjoy.)
- Front of house management, planning and organisation (cloakroom, float, health and safety, security, signage, staff, tickets, toilets, welcome / meet and greet etc).
- Front of house on the day
- Marketing and promotion
- Payments – how you'll take them and who's responsible
- Planning and project management
- Programming
- Stage management
- Venue / online streaming
- Add any other subheadings you need.

These are useful subheadings for planning your literary event. Making a decision about the venue (and whether to host it on or offline or do a hybrid event) and about the budget should happen early in the process, because you'll base the rest of your planning on these key decisions. Remember that you'll need a venue or venues from which to 'broadcast' or record your event if you go down that route, and you'll need to put someone in charge of the tech.

Remember to consider accessibility when you're discussing whether to go online, offline or hybrid. How will you make sure you reach as many people as possible and that the target audience can take part in your event?

A note about venues

Some pubs in the UK will give you a room for free as long as you buy drinks. Some venues will take a share of the money taken on the door in return for the space. Find out how venues in your area operate. Bookshops and libraries are also worth approaching. The alternative end of the spectrum means investing in an elegant venue and setting a door price that covers your expenses and allows you to pay your readers. Also, remember to check out booking services like EventBrite and TicketSource. There is usually a free option.

Strategic questions

Based on the typical format of readings, festivals and workshops you've enjoyed, answer these questions:

- Why are we putting on this event?
- Are we aiming to make a profit?
- Where is our target audience?
- What kind of writing will we include?
- Who do we know who will read their work?
- How many speakers or readers?
- How long will each speak and who will chair?
- Should we approach a publisher or independent bookshop to sell books?
- Should we do open mic? How will we organise it? (An open mic allows members of the audience to read their work.)
- How will we do it differently?

Action plan

1. Assuming you, or members of your team, have already been to online and offline literary events, including those in your local area, and have built some tacit knowledge, here's what to do next.
2. If you're hosting an in-person or hybrid event, ring or email three potential venues, or visit in pairs. Ask specifically about their pricing and booking policy. Note down the questions they ask, as these will help you to plan your event. If the event is online or hybrid, how will you organise it? What equipment will you need?
3. Contact potential readers, being as specific as you can at this point. Get in touch with people you know if this is your first event.
4. One week later, write a plan. Working backwards from the approximate date of your event, decide when your key meetings (with yourself or your team) will take place. Decide when your deadlines will be. Thinking about the best literary events you've been to, and go through each aspect (For example: Was it on stage? Were there lights? A microphone? Was someone on the door dealing with front of house? If it was on Zoom, was there a host? A waiting room? Was chat enabled? Could the audience ask questions?) and decide how you will do it. Use the event subheadings and strategic questions above and make notes, adapting to fit your niche.

5. Meet up with your team and write an action list.
6. It might seem odd to plan *after* contacting venues and emailing speakers, but now you're a week on from those initial enquiries, you should have some replies, providing additional information that will feed into your planning process.
7. Based on your plan, create a blueprint for success on one piece of paper and add your deadlines.

Marketing your event

In sum, you need to know the venue (online or in person or both), who will be reading, and the date / time. Once you've got your practicalities in place, here's what you can do to market your event. First, here are a couple more questions for you:
- Do you actually want or need to market your work?
- Who do you *want* to come to your event?

Your target audience isn't 'everyone'

Your target audience isn't 'everyone' or 'anyone who fancies it'. You don't want people who aren't interested to turn up, and that's way too broad a target anyway.

You've got to answer the question 'who do you *want* to come to your event?' honestly if you want to market effectively

Broadly speaking, your target audience is going to be people who are interested in the kind of writing featured at the event. Writers, editors, readers, and their friends. But it's time to uncover your subconscious intentions here!

Who are you imagining in that audience? Is the answer 'the same people who always come'? When you picture the event, do you think of an ideal audience that's made up of your friends and family, or work colleagues, or students? Will it be people who tend to hang out at the same pub or community centre? Or made up of members of your writers' group, or other writers you know? How will you encourage people to attend from outside your bubble?

What does your ideal audience member 'look' like?

Your audience will most likely be made up of the following people. Note that these categories overlap:

- People who love reading, including those who buy books
- People who love writing, including those who have been published
- People who love attending and / or participating in arts events generally
- Those who work in publishing.
- Those who work for literary organisations like English Pen or the Arvon Foundation or Apples and Snakes, for example.
- Those who work in or study writing-related fields: librarians, booksellers, English teachers, English, Drama or Media students.
- Friends and family of those above.

Tips for marketing your event:

Here are some tips for marketing your event. You may need to get permission from the people concerned before you start.

- Record a video of writers reading or giving tips, and post it on social media.
- Write a blog post about the event.
- Appear on a podcast and ask to promote the event.
- Pitch a guest blog to relevant organisations about your event.
- Offer to run a Creative Writing taster at a reading or writing group in return for a plug.
- Ask to speak at another event at the same venue.
- Create postcards with material from people who will be reading at the event.

You're aiming to get information about your event in front of your ideal audience or, to use marketing speak, you're aiming to send your ideal audience to information about your event. Include a website address, or Facebook event page, or EventBrite link, so people know how to get more information and how to book. Make this easy for them.

How do you find your ideal audience members?

Where are your audience? You and the rest of your team are your ideal audience members, so start by asking: *where are you?* Where do you hang out, what websites and social media do you tap into, where do you go for information, what readings and events do you go to? That's where you've got to start. Make a list. Target those places first.

Do you know what everyone at your reading will have in common, for sure? They all go to readings! (This might be their first one, but they're still at a reading.) After you've targeted the events / groups / places *you* go for writing-related reasons, target the wider spread of relevant arts events / groups / places.

Word of mouth

Word of mouth doesn't mean tell everyone, it means get the information out to the right people, to the people in your ideal audience. So, do this:

- As soon as you know the details – the date, time, venue and readers – go to readings yourself. If you can possibly fix the details three months in advance, do it. That gives you plenty of time to go to readings and spread the word.
- If relevant, organise the launch at the same time as producing the book we talked about in the previous chapter.
- Contact the organisers in advance. Ask if you can plug your event. Ask people in the audience to tell their friends. You can split your team up into pairs to cover several events like this.

Taking the word of mouth strategy further

The organisers of an existing event are likely to know people interested in reading events! You support them, they'll support you. Support them a lot, and show you're professional and friendly, and they spread the news for you.

You can get even more Ninja about involving 'influencers' like this. Invite someone you know is involved with another reading event to read at *your* event; they will spread the word for you, and it's likely their list of contacts will be more established that yours.

Consider contacting local writing organisations, small

presses nearby, indy bookshops and public libraries. Here's how you might approach them:

- Research organisations (and people within them) to contact. If you don't know any writing organisations, find a couple of writing magazines and / or their websites as they are a good place to start your research.
- Email to introduce yourself and asking if you can take in some flyers / postcards or send them the details.

'Make money selling cakes'

Marketing isn't evil or shallow. Sometimes writers are worried or hesitant about selling their event; they don't want to be pushy, thinking it's embarrassing to promote themselves, to blow their own trumpet, or maybe they are a bit suspicious of marketing in general.

I went to a conference a while back and someone there was giving out flyers that said 'make money selling cakes'. It was a baking franchise opportunity. I don't know anything more about it than that. But it struck me that it was a good example of marketing that isn't evil! The flyer was advertising a specific opportunity. It was obvious what it was, and clearly communicated. Be professional and you can market your writing event in a friendly and reciprocal way way.

Discussion

Once you've hosted your event, get together and discuss how it went. For a more in-depth group discussion, talk about marketing for writers and how you feel about selling yourself and your work.

Want more?

Take a look at these books on marketing for writers: https://uk.bookshop.org/lists/marketing-your-book

For more information on running online events, try Ben Chodor's book *Transitioning to Virtual and Hybrid Events*.

You may also like to research some of the speakers who appeared at the Kendal Poetry Festival's *Where to Next?* event in June 2021: https://www.kendalpoetryfestival.co.uk/where-to-next-a-seminar-hosted-by-kendal-poetry-festival/

Literary Programming can also be a career path, whether you work for a big or small organisation. Getting experience of arts administration will help you if that's the kind of career you're after.

Summary of 'how to organise a literary event'

Get a team together, do some research and come up with specific goals for your event. Decide early on what budget you're working with and whether the event will be online or offline or hybrid; if you're going to host an in-person event, make a decision about the venue. Allocate roles to your team members and contact those you want to read. Market your event by targeting the right kind of audience, using the resources available to you.

Works Cited

Chodor, Ben. *Transitioning to Virtual and Hybrid Events*. Wiley, 2020.

Tondeur, Louise. *How to Write a Novel and Get It Published*. Small Steps, 2017.

PART III

Living as a Writer

A Creative Careers Workshop

'To be nobody but yourself in a world which is doing its best, night and day, to make you everybody else — means to fight the hardest battle which any human being can fight; and never stop fighting.' — e. e. cummings.

What is this chapter about?

This chapter is for Creative Writing tutors. What follows is the outline of a Creative Careers Workshop that I have run several times with MA students and third year undergraduates.

Roughly speaking, the workshop divides in two. A talk on living as a writer, and a workshop, using small group activities. It takes about half a day.

As you'll see, there are several small group and discussion activities included. You can mix and match. For instance, I almost always include the small group presentations, but I've never included all of the activities. I usually get a feel for what the group needs as I go along.

The next chapter in this section is about how to find a

writing-related job. That could form a 'part two' to this workshop if you like.

Living as a writer

Talk about what it means to live as a writer and the kinds of skills and systems that requires. At this point I usually bring in the ten questions that Jinny Ditzler uses in her book *Your Best Year Yet*, and recommend that participants read it. A number of participants have thanked me for introducing me to them. On a personal note, answering the questions helped me to get onto my MA course and to get my first novel published. You can get a sense of the questions from the contents page of the book (using the 'look inside' function on online bookshops) to see if they would work for you and your students.

In the meantime, here are some topics you might want to discuss, as a whole group or in small groups.

- Making time and space for writing
- Systems such as task management and recording submissions
- Treating yourself like a business
- Out-sourcing / getting help
- Managing your time – a day in the life of a writer
- 'Going to work' every day
- Marketing yourself
- Taking on other work to support yourself
- Selling work in more than one genre
- The difference between writing, editing and research
- The importance of breaks, time off and 'mulling it over time'

- Reactions of family and friends
- The importance of regular contact with others
- Interacting with other writers / Being a 'literary citizen'
- Working with editors and agents

You may also wish to discuss:

- the practicalities of getting work published followed by Qu and A
- possible sources of funding and where participants can find out more (occasionally I had representatives from funding bodies come in and talk at this point)
- books, magazines and websites that give details of prizes, awards, bursaries etc.

Workshop activities

Use the following workshop activities to underline the idea that it is possible to follow a creative, flexible career path, and also to help participants to understand that freelance writing is like running any small business; similar skills apply.

Outlandish and exciting careers

Ask workshop participants to do the following:

- Write down a list of interests.
- Follow up with a list of the really good things about you.
- Write down the most outlandish or exciting careers and jobs you can think of.

- Discuss the outlandish or exciting careers in pairs or threes and pool ideas.

Hot air balloon rides

Pursuing any career which doesn't involve 9 – 5 with someone else promising you a wage requires you to be proactive. Imagine I am going to offer people hot air balloon rides whilst I paint their portraits. I might also do some aerial photography. *From leaving this room until my new business starts, what steps would I need to take?*

Sometimes I demonstrate this part of the workshop using whole group discussion and a whiteboard / flipchart at the front of the room rather than small group discussion, as it saves time.

Pick n Mix Activity

In the 'outlandish and exciting careers' activity, participants made lists of interests and 'really good things about you'. Follow that up now.

1. In small groups, participants look over their lists. Then they match interests and really good things to the 'outlandish and exciting careers'. For example, if one person has said she is good with people and animals, she might be matched to a job taking tourists diving with dolphins in New Zealand.
2. Each group picks their favourite then feeds back to the rest of the group. At this point I get the groups to come up with names for their 'team' and to appoint one participant per team as scribe.

Small group presentations

Participants come up with group presentations based on their favourite career from the previous activity as follows, with the caveat that no one has to stand up and present if they don't want to. Give out large sheets of paper and coloured pens, then set up the following scenario.

1. Just as they did for the hot air balloon rides, teams answer this question: *From leaving this room until your new business starts, what steps would you need to take if you were going to follow that career path?*

2. Ask each team to present their step-by-step plans to the rest of the group in an interesting way, perhaps with role play or using large sheets of paper and coloured pens, or collage.

I usually find that the small group presentations are the liveliest and most memorable part of the workshop.

The freelance life

What most people discover from coming up with a step-by-step plan for so called 'outlandish' or 'exciting' careers, is that they suddenly seem possible after all! In the discussion after each group has presented, apply these ideas to living as a writer.

Have groups work on a step-by-step plan for living as a freelance writer, using the same formula: *From leaving this room until your new freelance writing business starts, what steps would you need to take?* Discuss the results.

Two approaches discussion

Below are various additional discussion starters that you can use with workshop participants, either as a whole group or in small groups, if you have time. The first is called 'two approaches.'

Set up the following scenario. Imagine two different writers who take two different approaches to their careers. You could even asked two of your workshop participants to role play these two writers.

1. Writer one sits back to wait for things to happen. They've sent some work out and there was some initial interest in their work, so they've decided to wait and see if it gets published before writing anything else. They feel overawed by the publishing industry and, after all, if it's meant to be it'll happen. They're nervous about sending more stuff out anyway, wanting to get it perfect first.
2. Writer two is proactive. They've sent some work out and there was some initial interest in their work, so they've decided to write five more short stories and send them to different places. They feel overawed by the publishing industry so they've found a mentor at a local writing organisation. Even though they are nervous about sending more stuff out, their mentor has told them there's no such thing as perfection.

How does each writer feel? How are their approaches different? What are the pitfalls with each approach? What are the advantages?

Doris's dilemma discussion

Set up the following scenario. Doris comes to your house for a cup of tea and a chat. She tells you that she really wants to finish her first book but can't afford to write full-time. In fact, at the moment she hardly has any time to write at all. She would like to go part time at work. Childcare is also an issue for Doris. Her husband thinks her ambition to be a writer is 'cute' but doesn't take her seriously. What advice would you give her?

Let participants share their advice first, then talk about the pros and cons, but here are some possible responses to Doris's dilemma:

1. Is it possible for you to expand the genres in which you write? Would two well-paid nonfiction feature articles a month be enough to enable you to go part-time at work? Could you organise another part of your life differently (batch cooking your meals for instance?) to give you more time to work on your book?
2. Could you expand the art forms in which you work? Can you fit the funding opportunities on offer? If you currently write only fiction, could you design a theatre project as well, for instance? Think creatively with a broader remit than writing. Some other art forms work more readily as time limited projects and might be able to address specific funding opportunities more closely.
3. Almost every writer does something else along side his / her writing. Try to find a part-time job which you can do alongside your writing. It can be very grounding to have a job which is completely unlike your writing, uses a different part of your brain or body.
4. A number of voluntary sector and community organisations advertise for interesting part-time

positions. It is also possible to build up a portfolio of Creative Writing teaching (or teaching in your area of expertise) or go into arts administration, which might be more writing-friendly than other jobs. Other creative, flexible career paths include, for instance:

- photography,
- complimentary medicine,
- gardening,
- running a bed and breakfast,
- furniture making

Different hats discussion

Start a discussion about 'writers' hats'. As writers we wear lots of different hats: creator, editor, for instance, and there are times when you need to wear your administrator hat, this is when you prepare submissions, make phone calls, write emails and keep records.

Time and space discussion

Start a discussion about finding focus time. From time to time, we need to try to find a way to get away from it all: a writers' residency, a retreat, or an alternative community. Find sources of information on the internet and check them regularly, and / or subscribe to a writers magazine which has a good directory. You might be able to create a ready-made retreat if you can find housesitting opportunities. You might also like to research the retreats at Hawthornden, Arvon, or at one of the venues listed on the Write Life website.

Want more?

For more on writing administration and setting up systems, take a look at *The Organised Writer* by Antony Johnston. Spend time working through the questions in Jinny Ditzler's *Your Best Year Yet*.

Summary of 'A Creative Careers Workshop'

This chapter contains the outline of a flexible workshop I have run many times with postgraduate and third year undergraduate Creative Writing students, with the small group activities and discussion starters included. Decide which activities will work for your students and leave out the others. It's usually Jinny Ditzler's 10 questions or the small group presentations on 'exciting and outlandish careers' that participants remember most fondly afterwards. These elements give the workshop a different feel from the usual run-of-the-mill talk on how to get published.

Useful websites

Hawthornden: https://www.hawthorndenliteraryretreat.org/

Arvon: https://www.arvon.org/writing-courses/courses-retreats/

Write Life: https://thewritelife.com/writing-retreats/

Works Cited

Ditzler, Jinny. *Your Best Year Yet*. London: Harper Element, 2006.

Johnston, Antony. *The Organised Writer*. London: Bloomsbury, 2020.

How to Find a Writing Job

What's this chapter about?

In this chapter, I discuss how to find a writing-related job. Many job opportunities are not advertised widely, because of the expense of advertising, and this is often the case in niche markets such as the cluster of arts and writing organisations that occupy one corner of the charity sector.

Tacit knowledge of the sector / niche, and an understanding of the writing organisations in your part of the world, is therefore very important if you are searching for a writing-related job. Sometimes this process can feel a bit like a treasure hunt, because by visiting or researching one organisation means you learn about another, and so on.

Routes to finding a writing-related job

After searching the jobs listing, you have at least three additional routes to finding a writing-related job:

1. You can target a particular organisation,

sending a CV and asking if they have any openings.
2. You can look regularly on the websites of smaller organisations in your area of interest, or tangential to it. Try the 'about' section or look at the small print at the bottom of the homepage for 'jobs' or 'vacancies'. You can also check out the organisations followers on Twitter. You may find similar writing organisations that way. Crucially make this systematic, rather than ad hoc. Make a list. Check through your list on a monthly basis. Mark time in your diary to do it.
3. You can exploit your weak contacts.

Exploiting your weak contacts

The theory goes that we share knowledge and resources with our closest contacts. We don't have exactly the same resources as our friends, of course, but there is much overlap. To use a sociologist's terminology, our friends and immediate acquaintances are our 'social network' (not necessarily online) and we have the same 'spheres of influence'. Have a look at Christakis and Fowler's *Connected* if you like this idea.

Our weak contacts, on the other hand, are people we don't know as well. We don't move in their circles. We don't have the same 'spheres of influence'. In other words, because we don't move in the same circles, we have different contacts and resources. These are friends of friends or associates of acquaintances or work mates. You might be friends with weak contacts on social media, depending on the way you use it. You might want to use

Linked In especially for the purpose of gathering both strong and weak contacts.

A form of networking

Exploiting your weak contacts is a kind of networking and it works just as well for introverts as it does for extroverts as it doesn't have to involve chatting to people at a party! You may have heard of the six degrees of separation – the theory that everyone on the planet is only six contacts away from one another – whether that's true or not, the advice to 'exploit your weak contacts' plays on that idea. You can create your own network by getting good at exploiting your weak contacts. As I said, this doesn't just apply to social media – it applies offline and face-to-face too – but it's easy to see how 'friends' or 'friends of friends' on Facebook or other social media platforms will have their own contacts that they might be willing to share with you.

Find a reflexologist

Because your immediate friends know your friends of friends, you can draw on *all of* the information they hold and their 'spheres of influence'. You have to ask, and you have to be fairly direct with the people you do know. Try this experiment today: think of a contact you don't have and find one through your weak contacts. For instance, I don't personally know any reflexologists. Unless you know one already, ask your friends to recommend a reflexologist. Does the answer come from within your immediate sphere of influence, or from a weak contact?

By the way, it's easier to do this if you target particular friends to ask or a responsive Facebook group rather than putting out a general call. Often when we don't get a positive response to a request it's because we put out a general call, not because there aren't any reflexologists known to our weak contacts. This is because of something called Bystander Syndrome; essentially this means that everyone thinks it's someone else's problem. This is something Robert Cialdini writes about in his game-changing book *Influence* (2007). Your search will also be affected by Facebook's algorithms.

Once you've found a reflexologist, try looking for a submission or job opportunity in the same way. If you find one, please share it with someone else you know. (In other words, pass it on up the line.)

Niches within the charity, arts, or events management sectors

There are writing-related organisations within the charity, arts, or events management sectors. The smaller organisations might only be known by people within their niche.

First of all, the charity sector is a big one and is generally a good one for writers, because most charities will have websites or magazines or other communication channels in need of copy (i.e. text written to a brief) and they are likely to be approachable, especially if you have an interest in, or personal experience of, the charity's remit.

There are writing-related charities – often educational ones or literature development organisations, or organisations set up by and for writers, or all three. There are also a few with a human rights angle (such as PEN). These are usually fairly small organisations. Many, but definitely not all, will be in a big city. Some offer internships, voluntary opportunities, and writing residencies. Some have been going a long time, have lots of prestige and contacts, and are therefore a good way to find out about other organisations and opportunities; they can operate as a hub for you. Find out where your hub is situated. For example, here in Brighton we have New Writing South and Creative Future and Little Green Pig, for example, as well as several other arts venues and organisations.

Arts and Literature Festivals

Simply because there are so many of them, arts and literary festivals provide a great opportunity to get experience of arts administration, literary programming and events management. The famous ones are household names. At the other extreme, there's probably a small festival local to you that you don't know about yet. Some positions will be voluntary, but you can bookmark the website and check back regularly for paid opportunities.

Sources of information

You can start out looking in writing magazines (like *Mslexia* or *Writing Magazine* in the UK or *The Writer* in the US) and their websites. Go to events, pick up leaflets, go to festivals, look on the more established websites on a regular basis.

Check out any of the more established writing organisations, like Arvon, the TLC, the Poetry Libraries or NAWE in the UK. NAWE's Writers' Compass and Mslexia's directory of indy presses are good ways to discover small organisations that might have job openings. The AWP website is a good place to start in the US. As I've said before, I list some of these organisations in the last chapter of my book *How to Write a Novel and Get It Published*, including several international ones.

Social media

The world of social media is developing all the time and writing organisations definitely have a presence. Spend some time doing some research. Twitter and Facebook are also a good source of information but don't reply on social media alone. Sometimes it is hard a) to distinguish organisations that are reliable and permanent from those that are unreliable and impermanent b) to capture the rather transitory flow of information. Find the organisations you love, and check out their Facebook pages / twitter stream regularly, with the above caveats.

Visit / Research

With a couple of friends, visit a writers' venue close to you or research their online presence. Find a 'hub' for writers and writing organisations if you can, or a writers' / poetry library. Find out about readings and events and attend one.

Discussion

What happened when you searched for a reflexologist? Did you get any unexpected results? What are the pitfalls when you're trying to 'exploit your weak contacts'? How could you use this technique to find calls for submission (so you can send your work out to be published) or to find a writing-related job?

Want more?

Have a look at *Connected* for more on social networks. It's a fascinating read.

How to Write, another book in this series will give you

lots of writing prompts to use whether you're a Creative Writing tutor or student.

Summary this chapter

To find a writing-related job, you can search the jobs listing, target a particular company, and / or exploit your weak contacts. Our weak contacts are people we don't know as well as our friends, the equivalent of friends of friends on Facebook. Because we don't move in exactly the same circles, we have different contacts and resources. We don't have the same 'spheres of influence'. Unless you know one already, ask your friends to recommend a reflexologist, to test this out.

There are writing-related organisations within the charity, arts, education, or events management sectors. The smaller organisations might only be known by people within their niche. Because there are so many of them, arts and literary festivals provide an opportunity to get experience. Start with writing magazines and their websites, then check out any of the more established writing organisations. Try social media, but don't rely on it entirely. Visit / research writing venues with a friend to get a feel for them.

Useful websites

AWP writing calendar: https://www.awpwriter.org/community_calendar/writers_calendar

We love book festivals: https://www.welovebookfestivals.com/festival-calendar

Works Cited

Cialdini, Robert. *Influence: The Psychology of Persuasion.* HarperBusiness, 2007.

Christakis, Nicholas and James Fowler. *Connected: The Amazing Power of Social Networks and How They Shape Our Lives.* London: Harper, 2011.

Taylor, Debbie. *Indy Press Guide.* Newcastle: Mslexia, 2020.

Tondeur, Louise. *How to Write a Novel and Get It Published.* Small Steps, 2017. https://www.louisetondeur.co.uk/how-to-write-a-novel-and-get-it-published/

Tondeur, Louise. *How to Write.* Small Steps, 2017. https://www.louisetondeur.co.uk/how-to-write-writing-prompts

Acknowledgments

Some of the material in this book has previously been published and subsequently adapted, as follows:

'Watching the nettles', in Part One, Week Four, was first published in the journal of the Arvon Foundation, June 2005.

'The Green Machine', in the same chapter, is an adapted version of an article called 'Small Steps to Creative Learning: the Toolkit Approach to Creativity', which appeared in *Creative Teaching & Learning Magazine* in August 2012.

A version of 'Week Five: Creative Visualisation' first appeared in the journal of the National Association of Writers in Education (NAWE) as 'Creative Visualization', *Writing in Education*, 47, Spring 09.

Some of 'Week Nine: Mindfulness' and 'Week Ten: Can Creative Writing Be Taught?' were first published in the journal of NAWE, as part of an article called 'Learning and teaching creativity: asking how rather than can or should'. *Writing in Education*. No. 69, Aug 2016, p. 50-57, which I have adapted for this book.

Some of the exercises in this book were trialled in seminars and workshops for an undergraduate module I wrote and taught for several years at the University of Roehampton called *Thinking Like a Writer*. I first facilitated the Creative Careers workshop outlined in Part Three with groups of postgraduate and third year undergraduate students, hosted by Roehampton. I am grateful to my former students, workshop attendees and Arvon writers for all they taught me. Thanks, also, to my former colleagues Judith Bryan, Elizabeth Clegg, Susan Greenberg, Jeff Hilson, Peter Jaeger, Ariel Kahn, Leone Ross and James Smythe.

About the Author

After doing a Creative Writing MA at The University of East Anglia in the noughties, Lou Tondeur published *The Water's Edge* and *The Haven Home for Delinquent Girls* with Headline Review, did a PhD, travelled around the world, started a family, and became a Creative Writing lecturer. Since then she has supported countless numbers of writers through mentoring and editorial feedback. *Unusual Places*, her first short story collection, came out in 2018 and she is currently working on her next novel. Lou lives near Brighton on the sometimes sunny south coast of England, teaches for the Open University, and blogs at: www.louisetondeur.co.uk

facebook.com/louisetondeurwriter
twitter.com/LouiseTondeur
bookbub.com/profile/louise-tondeur

Also by Louise Tondeur

How to Write

Find Time to Write

How to Write a Novel and Get It Published

Drama Lesson Plans for Busy Teachers: Book One

Drama Lesson Plans for Busy Teachers: Book Two

www.ingramcontent.com/pod-product-compliance
Lightning Source LLC
Chambersburg PA
CBHW060526080526
44586CB00012B/631